While being no stranger  pets a message of uncomp Jim has mastered the art of sharing timeless truths in a fresh, compelling way. *The Rope of Hope* will be a spiritual lifeline to anyone going through a personal crisis. You will be impressed with both the wisdom and compassion with which he speaks. This man has a gift for healing deep, personal pain and releasing hope to the weary traveler.

Harry R. Jackson, Jr.
Hope Christian Church; High Impact Leadership Coalition

Dr. Jim Bolin has a word for all who are "at the end of their rope" . . . and it is not "tie a knot and hold on." He reveals the hidden resources that are ours in Christ Jesus. From the Word of God, Jim plumbs the depths of the original languages and brings to the reader a treasure trove of spiritual truth. He carefully weaves strand after strand into an unbreakable rope that will tie the believer to the unmovable throne of God. Here is a book that is a soul anchor in a storm-tossed world. To all I say, buy it, believe it and share it.

Dr. Ron Phillips
Pastor's Study, Abba's House, Chattanooga, Tennessee

Pastor Jim Bolin, in this book, definitively addresses the relevant subject of "hope." His many years of pastoral experience equip him to be personal, practical and powerful as he offers insights that are heartfelt and encouraging. I wholeheartedly endorse this book. Its readers will find it informative, inspirational and stimulating.

Donald M. Walker, Ed.D.
Administrative Bishop, Church of God in North Georgia

"This book does not contain mere information . . . It carries the promise of TRANSFORMATION as Bishop Jim Bolin awakens the most necessary ingredient for change . . . HOPE. Many books claim that they will change your life. This one will. Grab hold of the rope of hope and get ready to climb higher into your destiny!"

Robert Stearns

Executive Director, Eagles' Wings Ministries

At some point in your journey, you will encounter a particular passage that will be both challenging and daunting. Two things can happen, one of which will determine how long you are in that particular place. You will either go it alone as many others before you have done and come out of it—an explorer with many harrowing stories of the faithfulness of God. Or you will find someone like Bishop Bolin, a seasoned guide, who will guide you through the precipitous places without injury, simply because he has been there and has both the experience and wisdom to get you through. You will still have many testimonies of the faithfulness of God, but you will have fewer experiences that frightened you along the way. Bishop Bolin has fashioned his love for the Word, his love for God, and his love for God's people into a marvelous statement of the power of hope. Behind the whole statement is a life of worship and dependence upon God that authenticates the truths he shares with us.

Joseph Garlington, Sr.

Presiding Bishop, Reconciliation Ministries International:
An International Network of Churches and Ministries.
Senior Pastor, Covenant Church of Pittsburgh

The Rope of HOPE

Strength *for when you're hanging by a thread*

BISHOP JIM BOLIN

FOREWORD BY JOHN BEVERE

The Rope of HOPE

Strength *for when you're hanging by a thread*

 KAIROS PUBLISHING®

The Rope of Hope
Copyright © 2007 by Jim Bolin

Published by Kairos Publishing
PO Box 450
Clarence, NY 14031
www.kairos.org/publishing

Contents

ACKNOWLEDGMENTS

I wish to thank Robert Stearns, Director of Kairos Publishing, for his belief in this message of hope, and the team at Eagles' Wings for their unselfish attitude in helping me to bring this book to you, the reader.

I wish to thank my Administrative Assistant, Michelle Brown for her steadfast belief in me and her untiring work toward the completion of this project. I offer my appreciation to Dr. Justin Harley for his comprehensive research and development expertise. To Jared Jones, my Executive Assistant, I extend much gratitude for his watchful eye over the unfolding and completion of this book.

A very special thank you goes to the staff and congregation of Trinity Chapel, who have allowed me to lead them for the past 24 years as their Pastor and Bishop. Their support and love has been and continues to be living proof that hope is still alive and growing.

This message of hope has not been lived out in a vacuum, but in the living example of my family. To Jason, my son and Executive Pastor of Trinity Chapel; his wife, Sarah; and their two children, Jay and Caroline; my daughter Jessica and her husband Jared Jones and their daughter, Berkleigh: thank you for always believing the best in me, for standing with Dad and Mom in and through some dark times, and for being God's choice of the Rope of Hope for me on more than one occasion.

To Robin, my wife and best friend of over 35 years, thank you for never giving up on me, for always loving me in the good and the bad, and for being the picture of a living hope that stands when many have turned and run. Thank you Robin for helping to get this message of hope out of me and into a world that desperately needs to hear that God is not finished with us yet.

FOREWORD

When I was approached about doing a foreword for Jim Bolin's book, I was extremely eager to be a part of this project—not only because I respect Jim Bolin for being a strong, steady, consistent man of God and a dear friend; but also because the subject of hope is vitally important in living an effective life here and now.

While thinking on the subject of hope, I was reminded of the story of Sir Ernest Shackleton and the voyage of the *Endurance*. The early 1900s had brought about a great age of exploration, similar to the space race in the 1960s. It was the exploration of the South Pole. This cold, stark, lifeless landscape long had called to the adventurous at heart and Sir Ernest Shackleton, an Irish explorer, responded.

After several exploratory trips to the Antarctic, Shackleton prepared to journey across the Antarctic. After crewing and stocking his ship, the *Endurance*, Shackleton set off from England on August 1st, 1914. Five months into their journey and 100 miles away from the landing point, temperatures plummeted and the *Endurance* was frozen in ice. Shackleton ordered that the ship be abandoned and soon after the ship sank beneath the ice, stranding the crew of 28 on the ice, hundreds of miles from food and shelter.

For five months the crew headed westward, dragging lifeboats around the ice, avoiding crevasses and openings in the sea that threatened to swallow them up. But instead of making westward progress, they actually found that they had floated 30 miles east of their original location. Discovering this fact, Shackleton ordered the crew to float the boats and head for Elephant Island, an uninhabited piece of land in the Weddell Sea.

When the crew reached Elephant Island, it had been almost a year and half since they had last set foot on land. But if they thought the island would provide them with food and shelter, they were sorely mistaken. No vessels stopped at the island and a chance rescue could not be counted on. Shackleton knew that he would have to cross over 800 miles of open, dangerous seas in a 20-foot lifeboat in order to reach South Georgia Island and potential rescue. Through high winds, 50-foot waves, and bone-chilling cold, Shackleton and a hand-picked crew made land at South Georgia Island.

Mounting a rescue expedition for the rest of the crew stranded on Elephant Island proved to be difficult as ice kept blocking passage to the island. Shackleton finally reached the rest of his men after three months and they all were taken to safety. The amazing aspect of this story is that not one of the 28-person crew was lost—even in the face of rough seas, blizzards, low rations, and extreme cold! One word can be attributed to their survival: *hope.*

God has given you a dream, much like Abraham, and you have set sail on this adventure of life with high hopes of clear sailing and the fulfillment of that dream. Unfortunately, many times we are caught in the ice of life and our original path is crushed in the ice, leaving us gasping for survival. Our light turns to darkness and the chilling cold saps us of our strength. But what keeps us alive in these situations? Hope—hope that God is who He says He is and will fulfill what He started in you. It's hope that kept the men of the *Endurance* alive through trials and tribulations, and it's hope that will keep God's dreams for your life alive and well in your spirit.

I know that this book will speak and minister to you, and I'm asking that you would open your mind and spirit to hear what the Holy Spirit would say as you read the words on each page. For those who are only beginning their journey with God, I am confident that the words written on these pages will give you strength to accomplish what He has called you to. And to those who are within eyesight of seeing the dream fulfilled, this book will give you the extra boost you need to see it through until completion.

I consider it an honor to have Jim Bolin as a friend, and I hope that as you read these pages, you too will see that this is a true man of God.

John Bevere
Author & Speaker
Messenger International

PREFACE

Andy Dufresne, a fictional character in the movie *Shawshank Redemp-*
tion, found himself falsely accused of murdering his wife and her lover,
and was imprisoned. After experiencing much abuse and isolation,
Andy took hold of hope and planned an escape which required much
patience and diligence. Several difficult years later, the Warden learned
the truth of Andy's innocence but refused to release him. One night,
a seemingly hopeless Andy asked for a rope from his inmates. They
believed he would hang himself, but in the morning they discovered
that Andy was gone. Instead of using the rope to end his life, he used
it to tie his belongings to his ankle as he crawled to freedom through
a narrow hole which he had begun digging years before. Once asked
how he was able to endure the hardships of prison life, all the while
being falsely convicted, Andy confidently replied that there is a small
place inside every person that can never be locked away, and that place
is called hope.[1]

Hope is necessary for mankind to be able to envision the future.
Since the fall of man in the Garden of Eden (Genesis 3), the message
of hope has been essential for man's existence on earth. For without it,
the greatest joys and the most desperate pains of life would prove
meaningless. Over time, some have accused hope of being just an optimistic illusion, but its existence has sustained even the most fainthearted-
ed. Mankind continues to hope even when there is no rationale for it.

---

1 *Shawshank Redemption.* Warner Brothers Pictures, 1994. www.imsdb.com/scripts/Shawshank-Redemption,-
The.html

In his column, Dr. Paul Wong states that "most people take oxygen for granted, until they have problems breathing. Similarly, we don't realize the importance of hope until it is shattered or taken away from us."[2] Proverbs 13:12 says, *"Hope deferred makes the heart sick, but when the desire comes, it is a tree of life."* Dr. Wong continues, "Without . . . hope, all life withers away."[3]

"[We] need a hope that is stronger than [our] best strength, greater than [our] highest success, and bigger than all the world can offer."

The New Testament Greek words for hope are *elpizo* meaning *to expect or confide* and *elpis* meaning t*o anticipate, usually with pleasure; expectation or confidence.* Hope is the confident expectation of a desired future condition. If all mankind had to hope in was ourselves, where would we be? Dr. Paul Wong concludes, "You need a hope that is stronger than your best strength, greater than your highest success, and bigger than all the world can offer . . . You need a hope that transcends the present circumstances and physical bodies, a hope that is connected with the spiritual reality which endures forever . . . You need a hope that is based on affirmation in the essential goodness and ultimate meaning of the Source of life,"[4] who is Jesus, the Son of God. He became our door of hope and *"in His name Gentiles will trust"* (Matthew 12:21; Isaiah 42:1-4).

Hope is the confident expectation of a desired future condition.

---

2 Paul P. T. Wong, Ph.D., C. Psychology "You Can Hope Again" *President's Column*. International Network on Personal Meaning, Coquitlam, B.C., Canada.
www.meaning.ca/archives/presidents_columns/pres_col_dec_2002_hope-again.htm
3 Ibid.
4 Ibid.

Such is the mystery of a hopeful, optimistic attitude. We can have hope even when the world as we know it is changing before our eyes. We can have hope even when we are elderly and feeble—embracing a passion for life that leads us into a purpose-filled existence full of budding promise. We can have hope when our eyes are open to the possibility of rising up from divorce, despair, defeat, and failure. We can have hope even though we hit rock bottom, because we have sown seeds of hope. Everyone knows that when seeds are sown, a harvest is gathered. Therefore, our harvest is inevitable because our hope is in the Lord!

***God has a way of knowing what is in front of us
beyond our ability to visualize
because He has already walked out all of our days.***

As we turn the corner of a new season, historically as well as spiritually speaking, we find ourselves as individuals, the Church, a nation, and the world facing circumstances and situations we have never faced before. Many of us had such hope and promise when we stood at the beginning of our last season and many of those things we had hoped for came to pass, things that we did not even dream or expect. God has a way of knowing what is in front of us beyond our ability to visualize part of His plan because He has already walked out all of our days. Sometimes when things do not work out the way that we want them to work out and things don't change, materialize, or come through, we find ourselves entering this new season with a sense of reservation, fear, and trepidation. There is a hesitancy to get excited about what it could possibly be. We can even allow disappointment to turn into depression, despair, and mental and spiritual anguish. There is the tendency to just give up hope.

I believe we Christians are living in an awesome moment in time because we are moving into a season of fulfillment of what God has promised us. I believe the Lord wants to remind us that there is every reason in the world for us to go straight ahead. There is every reason in the world for us to move up, move forward, and to not lose hope!

I remember when the Lord first spoke this Word to me several years ago. I preached on "A Door of Hope." Recently, I looked at my sermon notes and noticed that I had spoken truths about hope that at the time I did not fully understand. I was speaking prophetically about this historical and spiritual season. Now I look at this message in a different light because we, the Church, are in a place spiritually that we have never been before. There are literally thousands of eyes watching us Christians. There are churches and people scattered across the landscape of this nation and around the world that are looking to us for direction. There are pastors calling, saying "I don't know what to do," hoping to hear a Word, to find a door of hope.

Let's take a journey—with hope as our destination. On our way, we will read stories about real people who, while facing hopeless situations, realized that Yahweh, the Almighty God had provided them with an opportunity to hope in their future. We will also discover God's promises of hope for us Christians today, the steps we can take, and the choices we can make, as the worldwide body of believers, as a local church community, as well as personally, that will ultimately lead us to the true hope of our destiny in God. Although the story of Andy Dufresne is fictional, its hope-filled lesson rings true. In the midst of our adverse and troublesome circumstances, instead of hanging on by a thread, we can choose to grab hold of God's "Rope of Hope" and be the overcomers God has called us to be in this world.

These things I have spoken to you, that in Me you may have peace. In the world you will have tribulation [pressure, stress, adversity]; but be of good cheer, I have overcome the world.
— Jesus Christ (John 16:33)

CHAPTER ONE
Hope...
America's Greatest Need

In Hosea chapter two, God spoke through the prophet Hosea to Israel. Israel was about to be led into captivity and experience a difficult time. They had rejected the warning of the Lord and had not heeded the pleas of the prophets. So, because of that, the inevitable was in front of them. God was using Hosea as His mouthpiece. This is what the Lord said:

> *"Therefore, behold, I will allure her, will bring her into the wilderness, and speak comfort to her. I will give her her vineyards from there, and the Valley of Achor as a door of hope; she shall sing there, as in the days of her youth, as in the day when she came up from the land of Egypt . . . for I will take from her mouth the names of the Baals, and they shall be remembered by their name no more . . . Bow and sword of battle I will shatter from the earth, to make them lie down safely. I will betroth you to Me forever; yes, I will betroth you to Me in righteousness and justice, in lovingkindness and mercy; I will betroth you to Me in faithfulness, and you shall know the LORD . . . and I will have mercy on her who had not obtained mercy; then I will say to those who were not My people, 'You are My people!' and they shall say, 'You are my God!'"* (Hosea 2:14-23)

The Israel of that day was not much different from the United States of America today. Though all the gauges of outward success seemed positive for Israel, underneath, disaster was lurking. The people of this period enjoyed peace, plenty, and prosperity, but anarchy was on the rise and it would bring political collapse of the nation in a few short years. Hosea described the characteristics of the social conditions of his day: corrupt leaders, unstable family life, widespread immorality, class hatred, and poverty. Though the people continued a form of worship, idolatry was increasingly accepted and the priests were failing to guide the people into the ways of righteousness. In spite of the darkness of these days, Hosea held out hope to inspire his people to turn back to God.

The question we must address is, "Will we the Church of Jesus Christ, be a door of hope to hurting America?" Our nation needs the message of hope that God still loves us and is not finished with us yet. The massacre in Littleton, Colorado at Columbine High School served as a wake-up call. All of the sudden, that which was a heritage to us, that which we loved and was sacred, the sanctity of our children was invaded. It is interesting that the columbine is a flower that blooms in late winter and early spring as a reminder that the long dark winter is about over. It is called by the locals the flower of hope!

So many people are hopeless. They come to church to find hope, but in its place they find despair, defeat, lack, greed, division, and anger. People come out of the world thinking that they can surely find God in a church. Instead of coming to a place of worship where God is supposed to be, they find written across many churches in our land today "Ichabod," meaning God has left (1 Samuel 4:21). Many people are coming to find hope, but in too many of us Christians they are finding us just as hopeless as they are. They are not coming and finding answers and solutions, but they are finding programs and gimmicks. They are finding everything but revelation, life, and understanding. God has a people, a corporate Church body of believers, who will not just prepare for Him a place of visitation, but who will *be* a place of habitation for the presence of God. God is looking for churches of hope to send hurting people so they can hear and see His love is available and practiced by His people.

———————

God has a people, a Church,
who will not just prepare for Him a place of visitation,
but who will be a place of habitation
for the presence of God.

———————

America's Recent History

Recent American history seems to reveal that God is trying to wake up this nation. The 1990s was a decade of incredible hope, remarkable opportunity. Yet we, the American people were being deceived by leadership, not only in the White House, but also in corporate America, about the reality of the nation's financial condition. It seemed that America was in a financial bubble, a fantasy of monetary security, thinking that everything was going just fine, only to find out that it was just a big façade, a bunch of inflated numbers. America hit a recession.

The presidential election of 2000 caused division in the people of our nation, revealing the different value systems we embraced. It also exposed the compromise that existed in the ranks of leadership during the previous ten years. Some Americans were feeling hurt and let down, while others felt a sense of joy and jubilation because of a change in leadership. The enemy was turning us Americans on one another, political party against political party. The stock market began falling and people were losing their retirement savings. Then, on September 11, 2001 America was attacked by an enemy at the Twin Towers of commerce in New York, and almost simultaneously we were hit at the Pentagon in Washington, D.C. These attacks revealed a picture of what *we trusted in*, our two places of strength—our financial system and our military might. The attack was something we thought we had insulated ourselves from that could not happen. The enemy thought he would bring us to our knees in defeat, but he was met with a determined president and nation that had hope and would not be intimidated.

I believe there is coming a generation and a people of God who will no longer trust in money and government. These people will trust in the Lord their God. We, the Body of Jesus Christ, are these people. Now is the time that we shift and put our focus —not on Washington, D.C., not in a Republican or a Democrat, but in the God of the Bible!

Continuing on, in 2003 our nation found itself involved in a war in the Middle East. Here, in 2007, we are still caught up in war. We may have gone into war for one reason, believing we would find weapons of mass destruction, but I believe God is using this state of affairs to accomplish a greater purpose in our nation than we could understand at the time. This is a set up, and God is going to show Himself faithful on our behalf. I believe with all of my heart that what looks like a mess, God is going to turn around. Instead of fussing and fighting, if we, the people of God, will pray, seek His face, and not let ourselves be divided, but be united and stand together, we are going to see our nation come through one of its darkest moments (2 Chronicles 7:14). This nation of America will discover that our hope is in God.

A year after we engaged in war, in December 2004, a tsunami hit in one of the greatest Islamic populations in all the world, Indonesia. Governments from around the globe began to try to help the people in this region. The United States of America even sent two of our own former Presidents to travel around the world petitioning to raise money, but another solution was taking place. All of the sudden, the Church began to step into her rightful place. Without an invitation and without fanfare the believers from around the world began showing up on the shores of Malaysia and Indonesia and other places, coming with food, clothing, water, medicine, and help. The native people of that area began to embrace the Christ of the Church. They did not know that Jesus acted this way. They did not know that Jesus could help them like this. Now, there is revival in Indonesia. There is revival in Malaysia. It is not reported on the news, but Muslims by the thousands are coming to know Jesus every day! This miracle is happening because the Church woke up from her slumber and began to give love and hope to a hurting world!

Then, another year later, on the Gulf shores of this nation, a tragedy hit one of our prominent cities. On August 29, 2005, Hurricane Katrina roared on shore and devastated New Orleans, Louisiana. Thousands of people, displaced by the storm, were scattered to other cities across America to seek shelter. The federal government tried to respond, but its answer was insufficient. This scenario was yet another opportunity for God to show up. What the enemy meant for evil, God means for good in order to bring about His desired end and to save many people (Genesis 50:20). Katrina revealed all the holes that America had in the political system. So while the politicians fussed and argued, Operation Compassion, along with many other community churches, began loading up truckloads of supplies and goods. The people of God began going to New Orleans to help build and rebuild the city, and so many are still going every month. Believers in the Body of Christ began to show up on the street corners of the 9th Ward, setting up tents and helping hurting people, taking them into homes and communities. The Church did what she was supposed to do all along, love.

All of these catastrophes are simply seedbeds for revival. I believe God is releasing a flow of His Presence to us, the believers of Jesus Christ around the world. I believe a season of miracles is in front of us!

God is trying to get His believing people in America to wake up. This nation is eerily similar to the place Israel found herself in the passage of Hosea 2:14, when God said, *"Therefore, behold, I will allure her and I will bring her to the wilderness, and speak comfort to her."* The reason He said that He would allure her is because Israel had played the harlot. She had substituted other things for God. She was in good shape financially, everything was going well nationally, and there seemed to be peace around her. Yet, inwardly she was falling apart. God was trying to wake up Israel to what was in front of her and give her an opportunity to repent, although sadly, she would not listen.

We, the believers of Jesus Christ in America, have also substituted other things for God. We have followed the route of Mammon or money (Matthew 6:24). We have been pulled on and seduced by lusts, hoodwinked by drugs. We have made unholy alliances and yoked ourselves with those who are not believers. I am not necessarily talking about marriages, but relationships. We wonder why our lives are a mess. Our Bibles have dust on them. Our prayer chambers have been turned into closets to hold other things than prayer. There is no need for one baby on the face of this earth to go to bed hungry. There is enough food to feed everyone. Yet children of the world, by the multiple millions are starving to death because of greedy, power hungry moguls who are holding on to control and power. In the stock market, all of the financial indicators at this time are at all time highs. Yet we are struggling. People, in general, are bewildered. These confused and frustrated people have found their way into churches around the nation. Now, the church should be a good place for the confused and frustrated to come if they can come and find answers. But when the confused and frustrated come to church and discover there is no clarity, no revelation or understanding in the people of God, who can these hurting folks turn to for hope?

A Picture of Hope for Hurting America

God says, although, like Israel in a time of plenty, He is alluring us. He is a God of covenant. He is a God of His Word. When He promised Israel that He would take care of her, He knew He was going to do it.

Israel at that moment in time had reached a place where God released her to pursue her own desires. She was about to go into a time of exile because she would not listen to God. God was telling Israel in Hosea chapter two that there was coming a time when He would allure her, to draw her back to Himself. He would draw her to the wilderness, to a place of isolation.

We will find our answers not in people, but in God.

Have you felt like you have been drawn into the wilderness, a wilderness of isolation, loneliness, despair? Maybe you have felt like everyone has left you and nothing has worked out like you thought it would. Maybe you have felt like you have been in this thing all by yourself.

Speaking prophetically, I believe God is bringing us Christians to a time and a place where we are realizing and understanding that we will not find our answers in other people, but in Him. God wants us to understand that there is one Truth, there is one Revelation, and it is Him. When we know Him, relate to Him, and commune with Him we will know everything we need to know to do what we are called to do. He is bringing us to a place of, what seems like, isolation in order to bring us back to Himself, to speak comfort to us. God is essentially saying to us that although we may be messed up, tore up, thrown down, discarded, forsaken, forgotten, feel like we do not have a future, we have failed and flopped, and nothing has worked, He is alluring us now! We are now entering a time where there is going to be a release of anointing, power and freshness that is unprecedented in our lives.

We are now entering a time of release of anointing, power and freshness that is unprecedented in our lives.

Hosea 2:14-15 states,

I will allure her and I will bring her to the wilderness, and speak comfort to her. I will give her her vineyards from there, and the Valley of Achor as a door of hope; she shall sing there as in the days of her youth; as in the day when she came up from the land of Egypt.

Here God painted a picture for Israel. In essence, He was reminding Israel that she had forgotten the time when she came up out of Egypt, when she had excitement for the possibility of her future. She had forgotten the time when she was released from bondage and despair, and how she came into a land of promise, a land of plenty. Like Israel, we, the Church have forgotten what God has set us free from, what He has delivered us out of. We have gotten caught up in the moment of plenty and we have allowed outward circumstances to control us. Spiritually speaking, some of us have just sat down and given up. But God loves us too much to leave us there. I love that about God! He says, *"I know the plans I have for you . . . plans to prosper you and not to harm you, plans to give you a hope and a future"* (Jeremiah 29:11, NIV). I believe what God is saying, in this passage, is that He will not give up on us, *ever!* He is going through these trials with us. Sometimes, we may feel like we are all by ourselves, but, even then, God is right there beside us. He has a plan for our pain, sorrow, and tragedy, and He will bring us out of that pain, give us a hope, and direct us into our destiny.

It is only when we, the Church grab hold of this hope, that we will be able to bring hope to this hurting nation and to the world. America has suffered greatly under the distress of the times. These are indeed perilous days in which we are living, but the true hope of our nation and this world is in Jesus Christ. Instead of allowing these times of trial and isolation to pull us away from God, let us allow them draw us into that place of intimacy with our Heavenly Father, so that we can fully live in the destiny He has planned for us. These difficult days are perfect opportunities for us to show the world that we believe and live what we proclaim on our American currency, "In God we trust." Truly He is faithful when we put our hope in Him. God is the hope for America!

CHAPTER TWO
Hope ... Heirs of the Promises for the World

In order for the Church to be God's hope for the desperate people of America and the world, we must know who we are and have a vision of what our future holds. God spoke through the prophet Hosea in Hosea 2:14-23, addressing the nation of Israel with His promise of hope for her future. In this chapter, we will journey through each portion of this passage of scripture to discover the Church's connection to these same covenant promises.

The Future Hope of the Church

Hosea 2:16, 17 states,

> *And it shall be, in that day, says the Lord, that you will call Me 'My Husband,' and no longer call Me, 'My Master,' for I will take from her mouth the names of the Baals, and they shall be remembered by their name no more. In that day I will make a covenant for them with the beasts of the field, with the bird of the air, and with the creeping things of the ground. Bow and sword of battle I will shatter from the earth, to make them lie down safely.*

Here, God was speaking through Hosea about three dimensions of Israel's future. He was speaking about Israel's present or immediate future, her distant future, and then her eternity, that which was out in front of her that will happen at an appointed time. In this passage, He was speaking about the millennial reign (Revelation 20:6), a time in the future where the lion and the lamb are going to lay down side by side (Isaiah 11:6), where there will be no more war. It will be over. We, the Church, have this hope found in the book of Revelation of the coming rule and reign of our Lord and Savior Jesus Christ.

The Hope of Revival in Our Generation

Hosea 2:19-22 continues,

> *'I will betroth you to Me forever; yes, I will betroth you to Me in righteousness and justice, in lovingkindness and mercy; I will betroth you to Me in faithfulness, and you shall know the Lord. And it shall come to pass in that day that I will answer the heavens and they shall answer the earth. The earth shall answer with grain, with new wine, and with oil. I will answer the heavens, and they shall answer the earth. The earth shall answer with grain, with new wine, and with oil; they shall answer Jezreel,'* **[which means, *the Lord sows*]**.

Hope is the confident expectation of a move of God to bring in the mammoth harvest of souls!

It is here that God was speaking about His plan for the future generation, our generation. He was describing a time when we Christians will call to the heavens and He will answer the earth. In other words, we will sow *petitions, praise,* and *worship* to the heavens, and the heavens will sow *answers, encouragement,* and *relationship* back to the earth. While we send up, God sends back with an answer. The *grain, new wine,* and *oil* are all pictures of *revival, renewal,* and *restoration.* When we sow into the heavens prayers, money, time, and sacrifices, God answers with revival. God is getting ready to pour out an unprecedented move upon His people. We, the Church, are coming out of the wilderness and we are coming into a season of grain, new wine, and oil. Hope is the confident expectation of a move of God to bring in the mammoth harvest of souls!

The Hope of Our Salvation

Hosea 2:23 states,

> *Then I will sow her for Myself in the earth, and I will have mercy on her who had not obtained mercy; then I will say to those who were not My people, 'You are My people,' and they shall say 'You are my God!'*

Here, Hosea was prophesying about a time years down the road when there would be a Messiah who would crawl up on a cross and bear the sin, sickness, and sorrow of the Gentile people who did not know Him (Romans 9:22-26). You see, Jesus went through what He went through for God's covenant people *and* for a people who were not God's people, who did not know who God was. Now, through our faith in Jesus Christ and our covenant connection, because we have believed, *we* have become the seed of Abraham (Galatians 3:29). We are just as much heirs to the promises of God as anyone else because of our faith in Jesus Christ. When God promised that if we sow to the heavens He will answer back to the earth, then it is not just for Israel. It is also for every single one of us in the Body of Christ. God will take care of Israel as He covenanted with her. Likewise, we, the Church, will be cared for and will not be left out or just take the left-over crumbs. We are blessed and we will be blessed. We will experience exactly what God says. Why? Because we have hope!

The Heirs of Promise . . . That Includes Me!

Hebrews 6:17-18 says,

> *Thus God determining to show more abundantly to the heirs of*
> *promise [**we are the heirs of promise**] the immutability of His*
> *counsel confirmed by an oath. That by two immutable things, in*
> *which it is impossible for God to lie, we might have strong con-*
> *solation who have fled for refuge to lay hold of the hope set before*
> *us. This hope we have as an anchor of our soul. Both sure and*
> *steadfast, and which enters the Presence behind the veil.*

Get ready! Get ready! Get ready! We, the heirs of promise, are going to walk into the hope which God has promised for us!
Prophetically and spiritually speaking, we have come through the dark
night, the wilderness. We have been out there with our back against
the wall, everything falling apart, everyone walking out on us, death
and destruction everywhere, but something is happening on the inside
of us. We hear the voice of God beckoning us to come near to Him.
He has a hope that is secure and steadfast. He has answers! We have
every reason in the world to move forward. We have every reason in
the world to get up and try again.

Hope in the Valley of Trouble

What is hope? Hope is the confident expectation that what God says
He will do, God will do. In Hosea 2:15, God said, *"And the Valley of*
*Achor, **I will give** as a door of hope."* What is the Valley of Achor? Back
in the book of Joshua chapter seven, Israel had just defeated Jericho.
God told all the people of Israel to take *all* of the spoils of Jericho and
give them to Him. Jericho was the first city that would be given over
into Israel's hand, and it was there that God reestablished the principle of the first fruit. He commanded the people of Israel to give Him

the spoils from the first city of conquest, then, He would give them the spoils from the later conquests. So Jericho belonged to God, but there was a guy among the people of Israel named Achan, who just could not understand why God would want all that. God does not need all that! My gracious! God has everything anyway. So really Achan's attitude was one of greed and distrust of God. So many times we Christians have this same mindset. We try to spiritualize and rationalize it, but we are simply saying that we don't trust God. We hold on to things because we don't think God can really take care of us. So, without Joshua or the people of Israel knowing it, Achan took and hid some of the spoils from Jericho's victory under his tent.

The nation of Israel then went on to battle the next community, called Ai, were defeated, and lost 36 men in battle (Joshua 7:5). When word of the defeat and loss of life came to Joshua (Joshua 7:6-9), he tore his clothes and wept. There was one thing Joshua did not do between Jericho and Ai. That was to pray. Joshua would never forget to do that again because he learned a very important principle: *one victory over here does not mean another victory over there, unless you talk to God in between.* Some of us have been guilty of this same mistake. The way God acted in one place does not mean He will act the same way in another place. It is vitally important to talk to God and receive His direction for the next endeavor. Joshua probably did what most of us have done, which was to assume that Ai was small enough to be taken care of without bothering God with the details. Some of us think we are smart and have it all worked out. We have our business cards printed up with our titles, and our big whoop-d-do, but we don't know everything and we need to talk to God.

So, the city of Ai defeated Israel and Joshua sought God. It was then that God revealed to Joshua that there was sin in Israel's camp. The sin of Achan and his entire family was exposed, and they were taken to the Valley of Achor and put to death. It was at this place that

God encouraged the children of Israel in Hosea 2:15 when He said, *"And the Valley of Achor, **I will give** as a door of hope"* (emphasis added). He told them that at this place of their trouble, their greatest mistake, their worst catastrophe, sin, failure, defeat, despair, and hopelessness, He set a door. He put a door of hope right in the midst of trouble.

If Israel had stayed where she was, without recognizing her need to hope in God's promises, she would have never received her destiny. Likewise, if we Christians stay where we are, living without hope, we will never achieve our destiny, our promise, our purpose in God. That is why it is important that we understand where we are and recognize what is in front of us. God has put a door right where we are. Will we stay on this side and die at the threshold of the fulfillment of all that God has promised? Or will we reach up and take hold of the handle and step through? That door we are about to walk through is going to lead us into a hopeful situation.

Hope and Faith Go Hand in Hand

When facing troubled times, do we have the assurance, the confidence, the trust, and the hope that God will see us through? Or is our faith in God shaken? Hebrews 11:1 says, *"Now faith is the substance of things hoped for, the evidence of things not seen."* It would seem that all we need is faith, but I have learned that faith is only part of the equation. Faith says, "I believe God *can*." Hope says, "I know God *will*." Faith believes, but hope knows. Believing is a good place to start, but even demons believe (James 2:14). We believe God *can* heal, but are we confident that He *will* heal? Are we expecting Him to? In the face of death, loss, setback, and tragedy, hope's attitude is, "I know who my God is, and I will not let this trouble keep me from my future." We must remember that our circumstances do not change who God is or what He has promised.

Faith says, "I know God can."
Hope says, "I know God will."

Many people have attempted to do things in faith, but when their efforts were unsuccessful they became disappointed and lost hope. When what they were trying to do, did not happen *the way* they thought it would happen, *when* they thought it would happen, or *with whom* they thought it would happen, they lost hope. Faith is the seed and it must have ground to be planted in for it to be nurtured and to produce—that soil is hope. **Hope is faith's soil.** True hope in God in the midst of trouble will cultivate faith to live and grow.

Hope stands in the face of the impossible
and is confident God is going to do
what He has promised.

Hebrews 11:6 goes on to say, " . . . *for he who comes to God must believe that He is and that He is a rewarder of those who diligently seek Him.*" Many of us believe God. We believe God can, but not many of us *know* God will. This is like a person who *knows* something, and no matter what happens, even if it seems contrary, their confidence does not change. Come what may, they will not budge. We all need to have that kind of hope, confidence in the rewarder Himself, to not move when circumstances are less than desirable. The *fact* is some of us don't have enough money to pay our bills. The *fact* is some of us are sick and dying. But the *truth* is, God is our Provider and He is our Healer. That is hope. Hope stands in the face of the impossible and is confident God is going to do what He has promised.

The Heirs of Promise Bring Hope to America and the World

I believe America and this world are so pressured right now, and just one event could pierce the bubble that is ready to burst. Our nation, as well as the world, is in great need of hope. They may not know what they are looking for, but we Christians do, because we know who we are. We are the heirs of promise and we know what we are supposed to be giving, hope. I believe God is saying to us Christians that this is the time for us to become a door of hope for America and this world. It is time for us to walk into someone's broken and devastated life and become the hope they need. God is bringing them a door by sending us, the believers with hope.

Just like the nation of Israel in the book of Hosea, we Christians and the nation of America have encountered a valley of trouble. In the place of our sin, despair, isolation, catastrophe, and war we have the awesome opportunity to hear God's Word, repent of our sins, receive His forgiveness, and experience His door of hope for our future. As the heirs of promise, we Christians can stand together in humility and prayer, seeking the face of Almighty God. He has promised to hear us and heal our land (2 Chronicles 7:14). America and the world have this door of hope. We, the heirs of promise, *are* their door of hope!

CHAPTER THREE
Hope ...
The Scarlet Cord

One of the greatest pictures of hope in the Bible is found in the book of Joshua chapter two. Let's set the stage for the story. The children of Israel, under Joshua's leadership, were camped on the other side of the Jordan River opposite Jericho. Joshua was a warrior, a captain, and a military strategist. When Moses died (Joshua 1:1-2), Joshua became leader of the Israelite people. God told him that everything He had promised to Moses, He would do for Joshua. He instructed him to go over and possess the Promised Land. However, before Joshua crossed over to the other side of the Jordan, God instructed him to prepare himself and the people of Israel (Joshua 1:3-11). So, Joshua led the children of Israel through a time of prayer and fasting. After this, Joshua and the children of Israel crossed over the Jordan, set up camp on the other side, and circumcised all the males who had not yet experienced this sign of covenant.

Before the crossover began, Joshua had appointed two spies to go over and bring back a report of the conditions of Jericho's walls. Why two spies? Forty years earlier in Israel's history when twelve spies were sent over, only two (Joshua and Caleb) came back with the good report (Numbers 13 and 14), so I believe Joshua decided to leave the ten negative folks in the camp and send two people over who had faith and hope in God's promise of conquest. So, these two men set out to spy Jericho.

An Unlikely Candidate Receives Hope

The two spies snuck in to the city of Jericho and found themselves at a bordello, in the house of a prostitute named Rahab. Now I know that is probably not where most of us think they should have gone, but that is where they went to hide. There are a couple of reasons why I believe these two spies chose to hide in the prostitute's house: one, because it was trafficked by a lot of different people, and two, most likely, it was a large dwelling that would provide a good hiding place.

It is very interesting that Rahab's bordello, a prostitute's dwelling was the place chosen to aid God's people in their conquest of the land of Jericho. In many ancient cultures prostitution was not looked at the way that we look at prostitution or the way the Bible looks at prostitution. Rather, it was viewed by many cults as something that was an honor. In fact, some Temple prostitutes were called "princesses" and were often considered royalty. Rahab was most likely looked upon favorably in the Canaanite community of Jericho. This aspect of the story is a beautiful picture of hope, because here we see an unlikely candidate to be the recipient of God's protection. This prostitute is probably one of the last people in our culture that we would pick out for God to bless and take care of. Yet God chose her, as one to whom He would bring protection and show Himself faithful. Not only that, He also chose to include her in the lineage of our Lord and Savior, Jesus Christ. Rahab ultimately became the great, great grandmother of King David and is mentioned in the genealogy of Jesus (Matthew 1:5)!

God accepts us like we are
and desires to take care of what is wrong in us.

As Christians, one of the problems we have is that we get hung up on who God blesses and uses to display His glory. Some of us think that if we can get holy enough then we can be worthy enough for God to anoint and use. Rather, God wants us to quit worrying about trying to get good enough and just come after Him, and He will take care of what is wrong in us. If we wait until we are perfect for Him to anoint us, then we will never accomplish anything of eternal value. God desires to take us like we are and begin the process of completing His work in us (Philippians 1:6).

The story continues in Joshua 2:8-11:

> *Now before they lay down, she came up to them on the roof and said to the men, 'I know the LORD has given you the land, that the terror of you has fallen on us, and that all the inhabitants of the land are fainthearted because of you. For we have heard how the LORD dried up the water of the Red Sea for you when you came out of Egypt, and what you did to the two kings of the Amorites who were on the other side of the Jordan, Sihon and Og, whom you utterly destroyed. And as soon as we heard these things, our hearts melted; neither did there remain any more courage in anyone because of you, for the LORD your God, He is God in heaven above and on earth beneath.*

It is evident that something was going on inside this woman's life. The Bible does not clearly say what was taking place. It does not say that there had been any kind of encounter between the woman and the two spies. But the dialogue and the words that she used and how she conducted herself with these men testifies of something spiritual happening inside her. She was not just a prostitute running a bordello. She was seeing something that the others in Jericho were not seeing. She was recognizing that the deity of the Canaanite gods that she and her countrymen worshipped was doing nothing for them. She believed something about these Israelites. This woman was about to experience something that would forevermore change her life and her position in life.

A Deal is Sealed with a Scarlet Cord

Rahab realized the favor being shown to her by the two Israelite spies and decided to engage in the deal of her lifetime. Beginning with Rahab, the dialogue between them continues in Joshua 2:12-21:

> 'Now therefore, I beg you, swear to me by the LORD, since I have shown you kindness, that you will also show kindness to my father's house, and give me a true token, and spare my father, my mother, my brothers, my sisters, and all that they have, and deliver our lives from death.' So the men answered her, 'Our lives for yours, if none of you tell this business of ours. And it shall be, when the LORD has given us the land, that we will deal kindly and truly with you.' Then she let them down by a rope through a window, for her house was on the city wall; she dwelt on the wall. And she said to them, 'Get to the mountain, lest the pursuers meet you. Hide there three days, until the pursuers have returned. Afterward you may go your way.' So the men said to her: 'We will be blameless of this oath of yours which you have made us swear, unless, when we come into the land, you bind this line of scarlet cord in the window through which you let us down, and unless you bring your father, your mother, your brothers, and all your father's household to your own home. So it shall be that whoever goes outside the doors of your house into the street, his blood shall be on his own head, and we will be guiltless. And whoever is with you in the house, his blood shall be on our head if a hand is laid on him. And if you tell this business of ours, then we will be free from your oath which you made us swear.' Then she said, 'According to your words, so be it.' And she sent them away, and they departed. And she bound the scarlet cord in the window.

The Old Testament word for hope is *tiqvah*. It means *to wait, to expect* from the Hebrew verb *qavah*. The verb form means *to be full of confidence, to trust in God's direction.* The original meaning of the word *tiqvah* is *to stretch like a rope.* It reminds me of a picture of someone who has been tossed out of the boat at sea in a raging storm, and someone on board throws them a life preserver with a rope tied to it. The person grabs hold of it and it becomes a lifeline. This is the picture of hope. Hope says that no matter where you are, no matter what you are going through, no matter what you are facing, the arm of God stretches out to you. The promise of God is coming to you. The truth of God is being revealed to you. Although the storm may be raging and your life may be a mess, if you hang on to hope and not turn loose, God will bring you through the storm. He will lift you out of the storm or out of your valley. He will do whatever is necessary for you to receive the fulfillment of all that He has promised you He was going to give.

Interestingly, the word *cord* or *tiqvah* here in Joshua chapter two is interpreted *line, thread, a rope.* Rahab was instructed here to tie a rope, the "Rope of Hope," to her window. The national anthem for Israel is *Ha Tiqvah*[1] *(The Hope).* Israelis sing the *Tiqvah.* They sing hope. They sing the song that describes the difficulties of the things that they have endured, how God kept them, and how they will no longer lose their hope again. They hold onto *tiqvah.* They have hope. In order for Rahab and her family to be saved, she had to secure the scarlet rope to her window and hang it out over the wall so it could be seen.

A Word of Hope to You

You may be in over your head. You may be standing in the middle of a crazy situation that looks impossible, but God is going to turn it around. The Almighty is throwing you a lifeline today, a scarlet cord called hope. Things in your life may look the same for a moment, but

---

1 *Ha-Tiqvah,* The National Anthem of Israel, adopted in 1948.
Words written by Naftali Herz Imber.

something changes when you have hope hanging out your window declaring, "My best is yet to come!"

This story of Rahab teaches about hope, about confident expectation. It teaches what it means to have a hope beyond the circumstances that are seen, beyond current conditions in life. Hope realizes that there is a plan that is greater than the present moment. Believe, understand, and don't give up, but hold on, and God will unfold it according to *His* time and *His* pattern. Stand in confident expectation, knowing that what He has promised, He is faithful to do. Remember, you are not just hanging on by any old thread. You are hanging on to the scarlet cord, ***the rope of hope!***

CHAPTER FOUR
Hope...Activating the Promises Part 1

In Joshua chapter two, Rahab made a choice for hope when she secured the deal with the two spies. She recognized the opportunity for hope for herself and her family and she chose to take hold of it. When we believers decide to walk in hope, five promises are activated in our lives. Let's explore the great benefits of these promises.

Promise #1:
Hope causes your enemies to be fearful and fainthearted.

When we have hope it messes with the enemy of our soul. Joshua 2:9-11 records Rahab's fearful words to the two spies:

> *We know that the LORD has given you the land because terror has fallen on all of us, and all of the inhabitants of the land are fainthearted because of you . . . as soon as we heard these things, our hearts melted; neither did there remain any more courage in anyone because of you.*

Rahab was simply saying that when the inhabitants of Jericho realized that God was on the side of the Israelites, they became terrified of them. The enemy wants to keep us hopeless. The enemy wants to keep us bound in fear and living in doubt, but the moment we have hope, the moment we dare to believe the Word of God, the enemy becomes *"fearful"* and *"fainthearted."*

Praise affects the atmosphere over your life, while hope positively changes how you view the circumstances in your life.

Praise affects the atmosphere over our life, while hope positively changes how we view the circumstances in our life. Praise confuses and scatters the devil. That is why every time we praise the Lord in the middle of our mess, lifting our hands in praise and worship, magnifying God, it causes the enemy to scatter. The Bible teaches that praise causes the devil to be hurled back and turn on himself (2 Chronicles 20). Hope sends a sound into the heavens that confuses the devil. When we have hope and hope is seen, it melts the heart of the enemy. It does not matter what the circumstances are or what the enemy says. When he sees our mind is made up, that we believe in Almighty God and we have our feet confidently planted, he begins to melt. When we have hope, we have a firm foundation. Hope speaks to our situation saying, "I will not be moved by what I see. My eyes are firmly fixed. I have the promise of God deep down inside me and I am not backing up." There, at the place of hope, the enemy's plan for us is being thwarted. We are reversing his plan to bring us down. We are melting his plan and putting fear in his heart. Hope is a powerful weapon, and that is why the devil is always trying to make us feel hopeless. He knows he is powerless before a saint or a church filled with hope!

Principle #2:
Hope is your reputation that goes before you.

Rahab made an interesting statement in Joshua 2:10 when she said,

> *For we have heard how the LORD dried up the water of the Red Sea for you when you came out of Egypt, and what you did to*

the two kings of the Amorites who were on the other side of the Jordan, Sihon and Og, whom you utterly destroyed.

Hope brings about a spiritual change. It also has an affect on the outward appearance and countenance of a person. Have you ever seen someone who has hope and expectancy? Their head is up, their gate is strong, and they have a confident look on their face.

We Christians should live and walk in hope. Our reputation of hope in God should precede us. When the world sees Christians coming their way, they should say, "It doesn't matter how bad things get. Hell itself may be breaking loose all around them, but with that Christian, it doesn't seem to bring them down. They always have a smile on their face and confidence in their heart. It doesn't seem to matter what they go through, they keep bouncing back and getting back up. There is something about them. I don't know what it is, but every time I am around them my life changes. I feel better." Hope is contagious!

Hope is contagious!

Our society needs hope. Our America needs hope. Our world needs hope. Hope should be dwelling in and coming out of every believer. But so often, we Christians are so busy being consumed by our situations that we forget Who our source is. We forget our foundation and Who has spoken a promise to us. I believe the Lord is saying to us, His people, that the character of hope should go before us and change the way the world perceives God. When others see us Christians coming, they will either have an expectation of something good coming out of us, or they are going to look at us and say, "If I could make a door where there *ain't* no door, I would make one right now. They call themselves 'Christians,' but they are the biggest sourpuss, negative so-and-so I have ever seen." What do people anticipate when we are coming into their presence? Is it dread and despair, or faith and confidence? We all have problems and need to talk and pray with each other from time to time, but that should not be our MO (*mode of operation*). That should not be what we are known by, but rather the exception to the rule of our lives. Our reputation should be that we have our act together, because our hearts and lives are locked into God, our hope is firmly fastened. Yes, we are facing difficult circumstances and are experiencing setbacks, but we know they will not stay that way because God has the last Word.

Hell shuts down when hope comes in!

A hopeful reputation prepares the way and gives warning to the enemy. Hell shuts down when hope comes in. The inhabitants of Jericho began closing the windows and rolling in the gang plank because they noticed the Israelites coming in with confidence. In essence, Joshua 2:9-11 revealed that terror had come over all the people of Jericho because they knew that God was with the Israelites, they knew that their goose was cooked! Instead of trembling at insurmountable, impossible situations, see it from God's perspective and let your reputation, one of confident expectation, go before you.

Principle #3:
Hope positions you for the right connection.

Hope, the confident expectation of a promised future in God, positions us for right connections. Rahab said to the two spies, "*For the LORD your God, He is God in heaven above and on earth beneath. Now therefore, I beg you, swear to me by the LORD*" (Joshua 2:12). This is where we are seeing a little more about Rahab's mindset. Notice the word *LORD* here is capitalized and it means *Yahweh,* the Name of God.

She called God *Yahweh,* a title not commonly used by someone who did not know the God of Israel. She realized that these spies worshipped a God who was greater than the lifeless, inanimate gods she prostituted herself to. This woman understood that her ability to have hope was connected to the God that these men served.

Many Christians are hooked up to the wrong things, putting faith in anything and everything but God. Their financial confidence is based on the stock market or on a raise from their employer. These things are all just resources. God is the true source. He will use whomever or whatever He chooses to provide for the needs and desires of His people. Many Christians do not have a clue that they are connected to God because they are not looking and acting like a person with hope. A person who has hope has confidence in their connection to God. They know that He is in control no matter the circumstances or the insurmountable odds.

Some Christians are connected to what I call *hope-stealers.* They hang around a bunch of negative, condescending, judgmental, pessimistic, "woe-is-me" people. They mingle with the "nay sayers," those who neither speak faith, nor live in and declare hope. They become so bound up and worried about their position and circumstances. In fact, many of them will go to the drug store and buy flu medicine before they ever get the flu. That is their expectation. They say, "It is flu season. I don't have the flu, but I had better get some medicine so when I get the flu . . ." They get the flu because *that* is what they are expecting. Hopeful expectancy has an affect on the body's physiological makeup. The hope of physical health causes the body to say, "Hey, someone believes around here, so I will function correctly." It is sad to say that some people don't want to hear this because so many like getting sick. It is the only time they get any attention. They move from one sickness to another because that is their level of expectancy. Let me just say here that I am not opposed to the use of medicine, rather I am against negative expectations. Hope-stealers are fed by negative expectations.

I want to challenge us Christians to change our expectancy, if it is not a hopeful one. Let's dare to believe that God has a better choice, and that choice is life! Who are we connected to? Our connection will determine what happens in our lives. As believers, we are positioned and hooked up to God, the right source. Let's stay connected to *hope-givers.*

Stay connected to hope-givers.

What was the color of Rahab's scarlet cord? Red. What is the color of blood? Red. What was the color of Jesus' blood? Red. The scarlet cord is a picture of Jesus, the hope of the world. If our hope is Jesus, then we are anchored. Hebrews 6:19 says that our hope is firmly secured and anchored in Christ Jesus. Whatever we connect and anchor ourselves to is what we hope in. Rahab realized that if she had any hope at all, she was going to have to be connected to the right source. She lived in the fortified city of Jericho that for all practical sense and purposes was impregnable by any outside force. Yet she knew that Israel's God had already given them the land. She believed that Yahweh, their God was also her source, the right connection for hope.

After exploring three of God's promises outlined in this chapter, we can see how true hope can be activated in our lives. First, hope causes our enemies to be fearful and fainthearted. Second, hope is our reputation that goes before us. Third, hope positions us for the right connection. These three promises provide us Christians with the necessary perspective for hope to be manifested in our lives.

CHAPTER FIVE
Hope . . . Activating the Promises Part 2

Remember the deal made between Rahab and the two spies back in Joshua 2:12-21? The two spies agreed to protect and preserve Rahab and all who were in her household from the impending defeat of Jericho, but the fulfillment of that agreement was contingent upon Rahab upholding certain conditions. Hope is conditional. As we look into Scripture, we see that the promises of God are "yes and amen" in Christ Jesus (2 Corinthians 1:20). With that thought in mind, hope is no different for us Christian believers. The hope God offers us is promised through faith in Christ Jesus. In order for us to walk in true hope we must be willing to activate the promises God has provided through His Son, Christ Jesus in His Word.

Principle #4:
Hope is conditional.

The three conditions for the agreement between Rahab and the two spies were:

1. **You must tie the scarlet cord to your window and let it hang outside so we can see it.** These two spies did not know God was going to bring down the walls of Jericho without a military conquest. They probably thought that when they attacked the city they would recognize the scarlet cord and therefore know the location of Rahab's house to protect her.

2. **You and your family have to stay in the house.** This meant that absolutely no one could leave the house.

3. **You have to keep this business of ours to yourself.** Rahab could share with no one what the spies were sent to do.

We need to think about that last statement. Too many of us are talking about other people's business. God did not call us to reveal everything about everybody. The spies told her that the plan would work if she told no one of this business of theirs.

It is evident by their confident speech that these two spies had faith and hope. These men knew who they were, they knew who their God was, and they knew they were connected to His promises. They believed they were going to win. The two spies agreed with Rahab that if she kept the conditions of their arrangement, even while everything and everyone else around her was destroyed, then God would not let one thing happen to her or her family. I believe we, the Church, need to begin acting with the same confident expectation as these men of Israel. It is time for us Christians to stand up, understand our rightful covenant and, with hope, declare to hurting people, "We are going through this together. In the name of Almighty God, you will not remain like you are, but you are coming out of this. God has better for you!" These two men understood covenant and dared to speak on behalf of God.

On the other hand, the spies warned Rahab that if she did not keep the conditions of the deal, then when God showed up, all bets were off and they would not be responsible for what happened to her and her household. Likewise, I believe God is saying to His people that if we will stay in covenant with Him, continue tithing, giving, praying, believing, seeking His face, and keep on doing the right thing when everyone else is doing the wrong thing, continue saying the right thing when everyone else is cussing like a sailor, then when all hell breaks loose, He will take care of us!

If we stay in the covenant, when all hell breaks loose,
God will take care of us.

Hope is conditional. It's simple; we Christians cannot have hope and live like the devil. We cannot keep doing what we have always done and expect different results. We cannot walk and live in hope, and talk any old way we want to talk, or think any old way we want to think. Hope is conditional, and as long as we stay in the covenant, like Rahab stayed in the house, we will live out our confident expectation. However, many of us don't want to hear about responsibility, about our part in the deal. We don't want to hear that we have to do something beyond just sit still and twiddle our thumbs. We must get in and stay in the fight. We have to stand and make the determination to not back up, to not sit down and shut up. Everything *for* us is in front of us! We must resolve to keep our eyes on God and move straight ahead. Isaiah 54:10 and 17 remind us of the wonderful covenant God has established with us, *"the mountains shall depart and the hills be removed, but My kindness shall not depart from you, nor shall My covenant of peace be removed' says the LORD, who has mercy on you . . . 'This is the heritage of the servants of the LORD.'"* We, the people of God, can maintain the condition of hope and stay in covenant with Him because God has promised to stay in covenant with us, and He always keeps His end of the bargain!

Everything **for** *you is in front of you!*

A Fixed Hope Does Not Change with the Passage of Time

It is interesting to note that Rahab kept the cord tied to her window for at least 21 days, from the time she and the two spies struck the deal, until the day the walls of Jericho came crashing down. It is clear that her hope was firmly fixed. She believed that if she did what she was instructed to do, then she would receive the promised agreement. God is not a man that He should lie rather He tells the truth (Number 23: 19). Rahab tied the scarlet cord to her window, which represented her vision of her future. We are not told how many times she went to the window and looked out, seeing no movement on the horizon. Maybe she even spotted the army of Israelites marching around the walls, but every time she looked out, I believe, she watched with eyes of faith and stayed in hope that what was promised her would come to pass.

When you look out your window to see what is in front of you, do you see with eyes of faith and hope, or with eyes of fear and doubt? If you have Jesus, the scarlet cord connected to your vision, you will see with faith and hope. This does not mean you deny the facts, but choose to believe the truth. Folks may say it is impossible, but the truth is, God can do anything! Are you seeing with faith or fear, hope or doubt? What or to whom your vision is fastened will determine what you see.

What or to whom your vision is fastened will determine what you see.

We all have opportunity to lose hope at some time or another. It is in waiting on the Lord that hope is revealed (Psalm 37:9, 34). Faith deposited in the soil of hope is the perfect combination for endurance. True hope is neither circumstantial, constrained by time, nor is it based upon our own conditions of what we think should happen or when we think it should happen. We do all that we know to do and understand that the power of life and death is in the hand of God. As believers, when we have taken our last breath, we have not been defeated, but rather, we have won. I believe that when we step out of this life and into the next, we will see that life in heaven is immensely better, so all is gained, nothing is lost. Let us begin to wait upon the Lord even in the midst of adversity. While we wait, we will mount up with strong wings as eagles and soar above our circumstances (Isaiah 40:31). God has a promise written on the wall of the waiting room of life, and it reads, *"For they shall not be ashamed who wait for Me"* (Isaiah 49:23). When we know who we are connected to, time becomes irrelevant and the waiting becomes an opportunity to rise above our circumstances because our future hope is in Yahweh!

Promise #5:
Hope in Jesus guarantees salvation.

This story has a beautiful conclusion. Rahab's connection to Yahweh saved her. In Joshua 6:15-25, the children of Israel, instructed by God through Joshua, marched around the wall seven times, on the seventh day. When the priests blew the ram's horn, the people gave up a big shout and the walls tumbled down. Now, there was a scarlet rope hanging outside a certain window because the woman Rahab lived in the wall of Jericho. The one part of the wall that did not budge was the section that had the scarlet cord hanging from it. I am reminded of the promise of protection of those who fear the Lord and abide in Him in Psalm 91:7: *"A thousand may fall at your side, and ten thousand at your right hand; but it shall not come near you."* The walls, everything around Rahab, were crashing. I will be honest with you. When the walls started to fall, I probably would have tried to find a way out. I would have wondered if those Israelite boys went back on their word. I might have questioned what kind of fool I had been to stay. But Rahab stayed, and when the walls rolled down around her, her home, and all who were inside, with the scarlet thread hanging in the window were saved because she built her hope on the Rock of Yahweh, Almighty God. It was as if God put His finger on that portion of the wall and secured it while His angels pushed the rest of the wall down. Then Joshua told the two spies to go and rescue the prostitute, her family, and all they owned (Joshua 6:22-25).

In the Greek, the word for salvation is *soteria*. Soteria means more than being saved *from* something. It means being rescued *to* something. Salvation is more than just *not* going to hell. True salvation means that you are going to walk in health, because the same word in the Greek is also often interpreted healing. In addition, soteria means peace, forgiveness, prosperity, wholeness, completeness, rescue, protection, and restoration. All these gifts belong to us believers because we are connected to God. When we are in Jesus Christ we have salvation and can absolutely know that our hope is secure as we walk out the conditions of the covenant.

We must stay connected, even when things don't happen the way that we think they are supposed to happen. The fulfillment of Rahab's promise probably did not happen the way she thought it would either. She might have thought that someone would sweep in and bring her and her family out safely. She may have had all kinds of grandiose thoughts and had no idea that she was going to have to stand when everything was falling apart and coming unglued around her. Had Rahab run out of the house when the walls began crumbling, she would have lost her salvation. The word to her was, stay in the house, so she stayed. She and all of her household were saved because she clung to hope.

When you dare to believe the Word of the Lord your hope changes your circumstances.

Grab Hold of the Rope of Hope and Let Your Hope Become Someone Else's Miracle!

Do you have hope? If you don't, a scarlet rope of hope is being thrown out to you. You might be living in a hopeless situation. You need the rope. You need hope. Have you received a promise from God that has not come to pass and things still seem really questionable, or things may have gotten worse? As you face life's circumstances, grab a hold of hope and dare to believe that no matter what happens, you have a promise from God and He is faithful to bring it to pass. I believe the Lord sees you and knows that you have been hanging on for a long time and not given up. His Word of encouragement is that your time for change has come. When you dare to believe the Word of the Lord your hope changes your circumstances. It is impossible for circumstances *not* to change when you believe God's Word! When you tie hope to your window, you see a good future and things around you begin to change.

Hope is persuasive. When you and I personally grasp this hope in Jesus Christ it will change us, and then others will see it and will want it. Because we believers link together to make up the larger Body of Christ our lives touch and impact so many others. I believe God not only wants to give individual believers a hope and a future, but He also desires that our personal life experiences cause hope to be birthed in the lives of others. 2 Peter 3:9 reminds us of God's compassion for people: "*He is not slack concerning His promise . . . and is not willing that any should perish.*"

In Acts chapter 16:25-34, while Paul and Silas were in the Philippian jail praising God, an earthquake happened and the prison doors opened. When the jailer realized this, he assumed all the prisoners had escaped. Fearing terrible consequences from his authorities he wanted to kill himself. It was then that Paul yelled out to him and, I believe, said something like this, "Hey, mister jailer man, we are all here. None of us have gone anywhere." The jailer man poked his head down the hole there in the inner cell and, I believe, replied in kind, "Hey! What must I do to be saved?" Paul explained to the man that if he confessed his sins and believed in Jesus Christ then he and his household would be saved. Not only were Paul and Silas saved physically, but a man and his entire family were saved from eternal damnation. I believe Paul and Silas knew something of hope as they sang songs of praise to God in that prison. They must have realized, through their ordeal, that God had a plan to deliver them, and had a prison guard and his family on His mind as well. We too should remember the value and future benefit of enduring our trials and difficulties with hope. We have dividends to collect in the form of lost souls!

God will not waste your pain.
Through it, He desires to save you and others as well.

Fathers and mothers, you better hold on to hope. It may look crazy for your kids right now, but *you* are their door of hope. Your little sheep may be outside the fold right now, but God will bring them back to Himself because you *and* your household will be saved. Pastors and leaders, hold on, stand firm. There is a door of hope, a rope of hope in front of you. You cannot give up because too many precious people are following you. Paul and Silas did not run out of their situation when they had the chance because they realized their salvation was not just about them, but it was about others as well. God will not waste any of your pain. Through it, He desires to save you and others. **Your obedience to walk in hope will become someone else's miracle!**

In this chapter, we have discovered two additional promises of God concerning hope. First, hope is conditional, based upon our agreement with and faith in the Word of God. Second, hope in Jesus Christ guarantees salvation, not only for us, but for the future family of God. Just like adding warm water to yeast activates its potential to leaven a loaf of bread, even so we Christians, being empowered by the Holy Spirit, are to implement and live by faith the active, living Word of God. His promises to us are real, ready and waiting to be activated!

CHAPTER SIX
Hope...
I Can See Clearly Now

The window to which Rahab secured the scarlet cord and out of which she peered is a type and shadow of the way she viewed her life. Her hope was securely fastened to the window, her vision for the future. Hope is the confident expectation of a desired future. The word expectation implies looking forward. Looking ahead with hopeful expectancy is vision, and vision is a key component in securing hope.

Vision is a key component in securing hope.

Defining Vision and Exploring its Purpose

The word *vision* is an interesting word because its meanings are complex. It is *the act of seeing external objects; seeing something outside of yourself, beyond yourself; actual sight.*[1] Yet, another definition describes vision as *something imagined to be seen, though not real.* This is pie-in-the-sky thinking or a *fanciful vision.* A further description expresses vision as *a revelation from God, the act of seeing or the ability to see.* In other words, it is not fanciful vision; rather, it means that what we are seeing is real. When we know what we see is of God, we believe it with all of our heart. It is true and genuine sight. This is a *faithful vision.* It is the vision we have that no one else sees or understands. It is God letting

---

1 Noah Webster, *First Edition of An American Dictionary of the English Language* (Foundation for American Christian Education, San Fransisco, California, 2000).
N. Webster, *New Webster Dictionary* (Lexicon Publications, New York, New York, 1990).

us see His intent and purpose for our life. If we don't have a faithful vision, we don't know where we are going, we don't know our purpose, and we don't understand why we are even here. We must have a faithful kind of vision.

Let us take a look at Proverbs 29:18 from the perspectives of four different translations:

> *"Where there is no **revelation**, the people cast off restraint. But happy is he who keeps the law."* (New King James Version)

> *"Where there is no **prophecy**, the people cast off restraint. But blessed is he who keeps the law."* (Revised Standard Version)

> *"Where there is no **vision**, the people are restrained. But happy is he who keeps the law."* (New American Standard Version)

> *"When the people do not accept **divine guidance**, they run wild. But whoever obeys the law is happy."* (New Living Translation)

Four words or terms are used here: *revelation, prophecy, vision* and *divine guidance*. All of these address how we view and respond to the possibilities of our future. Each of these refers to a future condition. They paint a picture of possibility. They speak of the window through which we believers look and see, with confident expectation, the hope we know we have in Christ Jesus. It is our view. All of life has prepared us to see what we are seeing right now. We have not gone through all that we have gone through, faced what we have faced, nor tried to overcome what we are trying to overcome without it affecting our view. These life experiences shape and mold the way we view life and that view becomes the expectation of our future. A confident future is founded upon the promises of God, and it creates within us an expectation that where we are is not where we are going to stay. God has something better in store for us. With hope, we must be willing to release what is *good* so that we can go on for what is *better*, and believe God for the *best*. This is what confident expectation does in and through us.

A confident expectation says,
"Where you are is not where you are going to stay!"

True Vision Reveals Trust in God

Our view, our confident expectation and faith in God reveal what we trust in. To look forward, toward our future, and to believe in our potential and possibility in God is also to trust. True vision is to trust God that He is going to take care of and provide for us. It is to trust God that He will give the strength, the wisdom, the connections, and all that is needed to accomplish all He has called us to do. True vision demands that we trust God because if we lean on our own understanding we will not make it to the destination He has planned for us. If we trust in the Lord in *all* of our ways, Proverbs 3:5, 6 says, He will straighten our paths and make the crooked places straight for us to walk.

Proverbs 29:18 says that without vision people perish. In other words, without true vision and trust in God, man will fall apart. One Bible translation states that people "run wild" without it, they cast off restraint, do anything, act any way, and go any direction, making a mess of life. So many folks have lived life that way. Even we Christians have lived helter-skelter, chaotic, crazy lives. God desires to bring order and direction to our lives, to help us see again. We need true vision so that we can trust Him to live our lives according to His plan.

What is in your vision?

As I observe people around me, other ministries, materials I have read, and even my own life, I believe we Christians make two mistakes concerning vision: we have a fearful vision or we have a fanciful vision. Let's examine these two blunders to determine what our personal visions are and how we might change them to effectively implement God's promises in our lives, thereby giving us hope!

Mistake #1:
Having a Fearful Vision

One reason we Christians do not have a hopeful and faithful vision is that some of us are just afraid to see. Fear can take on different forms: fear of change, fear of uncertainty, fear of having to give up something, or fear of failure. Any and all of these fears can immobilize and prevent us from moving forward with a hopeful and faithful vision.

Having a hopeful vision demands we change. In other words, we cannot stay where we are, like we are, because the God-given vision will require change as a response. It is that change which, for most, creates fear and uncertainty. We play the "What if?" game. We are afraid because we do not really know what tomorrow holds. We don't really know *how* it will all work out. Many of us have received a vision from God and later realized that He did not tell us everything we would go through to get from the starting place to the place of fulfillment. Sometimes the fear of the unknown disables us from moving forward and changing.

True vision lays demands on our lives. It challenges us and evokes questions about who we are, what we are doing, and what our purpose is. It costs us something. There is sacrifice involved in order for the vision to come to fruition. If we are not willing to pay the cost then the vision will do us no good. Because these opportunities for change are uncomfortable, many of us become afraid of having a vision.

Many people have a fearful vision because having a true vision requires responsibility. When a person has a vision, they are responsible to walk it out. Some people are afraid of taking steps toward their vision because they are afraid of failing. Some never even set out after their vision because of the fear of failure. Yet others attempted it but it did not work out. The vision is still inside of them, but the fear of failing at it again is greater than the desire to pursue it once more, so they back up and are powerless because of fear. Some folks are afraid because their vision may not work out and they have to take responsibility for what went wrong.

I believe the reason a lot of churches never go on to do great things is because many of the leaders in the church are afraid to take the risk of trusting God. Trusting God is really not a risk. It is just a calculated step of faith. We don't have to understand everything in order to take the step because we know who our God is, and we know if He said it then He is going to take care of it; although He may not take care of it the way that we think He will. The vision may not unfold how we think it should unfold, but if we keep our eyes on God, eventually He will bring us to that place of completion, and we will see it. We will experience it. It will come to life.

What kind of vision do you have? Is it a fearful one? Maybe you are fearful of having a vision from God because you cannot believe that God can do through you what He has put in you to do. Perhaps you had a vision and attempted to move ahead with it but it didn't work out, or someone spoke negatively about you or your vision, which caused you to stop in your pursuit. When you have a true vision from God you cannot stop. That vision will wake you up at night. It will follow you. Have you ever been stalked by the will of God or by a vision from God? If you have, even if you attempt to cover it up, God's vision will not leave you alone because God loves you too much to leave you where you are and for you not to fulfill His purpose in you.

Mistake #2: Having a Fanciful Vision

Another reason we Christians do not have a hopeful vision is because we are fanciful in our seeing. Now what does that mean? Let me explain. Being "fanciful in our seeing" means to be unrealistic. Some of us have visions that God is not within a million miles of. For example, some have visions of having a great singing career but cannot sing. Others have fanciful visions of being a cheerful greeter in the church but have the personality of a wall. Hello. Fanciful visions are visions that we are not gifted for, things that God has not spoken to us, but because we see a gifting or a calling in someone else, we really want what they have, so we start seeing their vision. It is really not something that is going to happen. It is just a fanciful vision. It is attributing to God what is not from Him. It is saying that God gave us the vision when, in reality, He didn't.

Fanciful vision is fed by ego.

As a pastor, I am sometimes placed in an awkward position when people come to me and say, "God told me . . ." I cannot argue with them. I just have to pray for them and let them do what they believe God has told them to do. Then, when they discover that their vision is not from God, I am just there to love them and help them begin the process of learning from it. There are so many gifts and talents. God has uniquely created every Christian and has designed distinctive gifts for each one. Therefore, believers should never play the comparison game and have a fanciful vision.

Also, I think one of the great reasons for this fanciful vision is *ego*. People sometimes say to me, "I want a church like Trinity Chapel. I want the anointing that you have." I wonder to myself whether or not they want to walk in my shoes, or go through what I have gone through to be where I am and where our congregation is. Much prayer, sacrifice, and change has accompanied this journey. So many of us Christians want the recognition, but are not willing to pay the price. We want someone else to pay the price and we get the applause. Ego gets the best of us and mars our vision. It confuses us so that we cannot see truth and reality. Our fleshly nature gets in the way because we want the attention. This type of fanciful vision fed by ego is not a God-vision.

When we fall into this type of thinking, we set ourselves up for a lot of pain, disappointment, and offense because we will get offended. There will be people who will outwardly smile at us, while some will insult us to our faces and it will hurt. A fanciful vision will inevitably lead to failure and disappointment. In order for us to move on into a hopeful future, we need to find another way to see!

A faithful vision is true to God and true to ourselves.

We Need a Faithful Vision

The truth of the matter is that we all have a vision and we are all going to end up somewhere, so it behooves us to have a *faithful vision*. If we don't want a fearful vision or a fanciful vision, then we must have a faithful one. A faithful vision is one that is *true to God and true to ourselves*. It is a vision that is *of* God and it is equipped *by* God so it can be done *for* God's glory and for our good. It is in our spiritual DNA, what we were made for. It means that we are engaged in walking out what God has called us to do and be.

Faithful Vision is Clear Vision

A faithful vision, one true to God and true to ourselves, becomes a vision of purpose and a vision of *clarity*. I believe that clarity is an optimum word that we Christians should embrace and begin declaring over our lives by faith. Even when we are not seeing clearly, we can begin to declare, "I have eyes to see and ears to hear, so I will see, I will hear, and I will have the courage to walk out this vision. I see by faith, and I have vision and purpose."

Clear Vision Brings Courage

Along with a clear vision comes the courage to follow through on it. If we really believe that we can do what God has called us to do then we believe that our life is going to make a difference; that we are going to matter, and something useful for the kingdom of God is going to flow through us. Hope is made of a faithful vision that sees a confident future and is fastened to the plan of God. When you have this clear vision, courage rises up inside of you and gives you the power to stand in difficult times.

God is in the Details!

Vision gives meaning to otherwise meaningless details. Without vision, one can become weary in well doing. Take for example the word picture of a community experiencing heavy rains and facing certain devastation if its earthen dike is not reinforced. If someone in the town does not do something about it, the town will flood and be destroyed. Every resident is asked to fill a bag with sand in order to strengthen the dike. The chore of filling a bag with sand would seem meaningless if there were no need for it. There is a difference in just filling bags of sand and filling bags of sand to save your town. The vision gives meaning to the task at hand.

I am reminded of a time when I went through boot camp. During one particular task our squad captains took our squadron to an area where a clothesline pole made out of big, fat steel and about ten feet tall stood with another large piece of steel welded to the top of it. The captains instructed us to saw off the right and left arms of the steel pole at the joint of the two pieces so all that was left standing was the long pole. However, they only gave us a hacksaw without a handle, just the blade. We sat outside all day long, sawing off these poles. It seemed like an exercise in futility because we did not know *why* we were doing it. Similarly, when we Christians know why we do what we do for God, then all of a sudden, the mundane minutia of a day, in light of God's will and plan for our life, begins to have purpose and meaning. All of a sudden, we are not just filling bags of sand, we are saving a town. We are doing something that, although in the natural looks pointless, will bring about a meaningful result.

Persevere in Pursuit of Your Vision

If you have ever gone to school, you may remember sitting in a class, wondering what that subject has to do with you or your dream. The pursuit of achieving a college or tech school degree or an educational certificate demands commitment to persevere through sometimes tedious studies and circumstances. The only thing that will keep you moving forward toward the goal of completion is having a vision of why you are doing what you are doing.

The reason so many of us Christians are confused and apathetic in our thinking is because we don't know why we are supposed to fight the good fight of faith. We really don't know why we are called to stand and not be moved. We need to understand that everything *for* us is in front of us. When we do, then the day-to-day routine of praying, reading the Word, and being faithful will not just be an exercise of futility, but will give us reason, purpose, and meaning.

The Benefits of Having a Clear and Faithful Vision

I believe we Christians are standing at the beginning of a brand new spiritual season. If, in this season, we have no vision for our future, then *that* is our vision—nothing—and we are accomplishing it. Spiritually speaking, without a faithful vision we will not go anywhere, do anything, or see increase in our lives. This absence of vision is our vision. Since we know we cannot stay where we are, it benefits us to go in the direction God has planned for us. Let's be a people with a clear and faithful vision.

Once we have a faithful vision for our lives, we can see God's plan unfold for us and also for those around us. Moms and dads must have vision for their families. Pastors must have vision for their congregations. God will cause our individual visions to unite so that we see love, acceptance, and forgiveness come to life in our communities, America, and this world. Our faithful vision is not just about us. It always partners with a grander purpose, something greater than we are. If our vision is only about us, then it is not of God. If our vision is only about us being seen, heard, or applauded, and people seeking out our business card, wanting us to sign their book, it is not of God. People may indeed want us to sign their book, but we will know why we have done what we have done; it will be because it was God's purpose and for His glory. Then others will be blessed.

We must have a vision, and not just any old vision. Fearful visions and fanciful visions just won't do. Our vision must be a clear, faithful vision in God and His promises for us. This type of vision will be the secure window to which our hope is fastened.

Do you desire change for your life? Do you want a greater tomorrow and a brighter season in front of you? You must have a clear and faithful vision. See yourself beyond where you are. See what God is doing in your life. Talk to folks around you and see what they are saying about you. Listen to godly counsel. But when all is said and done, begin taking steps toward what you believe is God's vision for you. If you see with fear or unrealistic expectations that are not of God, then stop and ask God what is His vision for your life. God will reveal it to you because it is not His will that anyone fails. Seek to have God's faithful vision for your life, one that will bring true hope to you and to those around you.

CHAPTER SEVEN
Hope ...
Walking Out Your Vision

The purpose of this chapter is to provide helpful insights for walking out a God-given, hope-filled vision on a daily basis. Some Christians don't have a problem with having a faithful vision. Instead, we sometimes find that it is more difficult to carry out the daily routines of life. We have a hopeful vision but we still have to take out the garbage and clean the commode! In truth and in reality, we must be able to walk out our faithful vision successfully and with purpose.

When you view your routines
through the lens of a God-given purpose,
suddenly everything looks different.

When we view our daily routines through the lens of a God-given purpose, suddenly everything looks different. Viewing life from God's perspective brings our world into focus. It brings order to chaos. God does not want His children walking in the dark. This is why He sent His Son, Jesus, as the Light of the world (John 1:9). He is in the business of bringing revelation to us. I have discovered four essential benefits that this clear and hopeful vision weaves into our daily lives. Let's take a look and see!

Essential Benefit #1:
Vision Keeps You Passionate

The first essential benefit of having a hope-filled vision is it keeps us passionate. A clear, focused vision allows us to experience ahead of time the emotions associated with an anticipated future. These emotions serve to reinforce our commitment to the vision by providing a sneak preview of things to come. If we know that what we are doing is going to ultimately lead to something that is finished, we will have passion to complete it.

Passion has played an important role in my life. I remember sitting at the computer, writing and typing my first book, *Recognizing the Spirits that Hinder the Flow of God.*[1] In my mind's eye I began to visualize the book completed and in the hands of pastors and people around the nation, helping them gain the understanding of why they are going through some of their difficulties so they don't have to suffer any longer. That vision pushed me. It was my passion.

Revelation 2:1-5 reveals an example of why passion is important. It prophetically describes a future time when Jesus is writing to the Church at Ephesus. He tells them that He knows their works, how they don't tolerate evil, how they have persevered and have patience. Nevertheless He makes note of the one thing they have lost, passion for their first love. They have lost the reason for their focus, the reason why they do what they do. Likewise, when we believers know why we are doing what we are doing, that long-term hopeful vision keeps the passion burning in our lives. We must remind ourselves of our vision, our passion, to push us through what we sometimes see as tedious responsibilities. Hopeful vision affords us passion, and this passion keeps us faithful to the task.

1 Bishop Jim Bolin, *Recognizing the Spirits That Hinder the Flow of God,* (Jim Bolin Ministries, 2003).

Essential Benefit #2:
Vision Keeps You Motivated

The second essential benefit of a hope-filled vision is that it causes us to stay motivated. Vision is the reason why we complete something. It is our motivation. For those who have been to college, the motivation is earning that degree, and not just the degree itself, but also what the degree signifies, a potential career opportunity. For some folks, the motivation is to master a trade and achieve a certificate that will open up new prospects at work for increase in position and in pay. It is that motivation that gives meaning. The end goal drives us to finish, it is our motivation. So many people have great ideas and wonderful starts, but they don't finish. Many churches today are filled with people who have incredible dreams, awesome visions, and great talents and gifts, but the visions never come to completion because they don't stay motivated to finish what God has put in them to do. We need hope-filled vision that motivates us to persevere to the finish line.

Essential Benefit #3:
Vision Gives You Direction

The third essential benefit of having a hope-filled vision is direction. Vision is like a roadmap. It simplifies the decision-making process. Anything in life that moves us closer to our vision gets a green light. Everything else is approached with caution. Vision prioritizes our values, brings what is important to the surface, and weeds out anything that stands in our way. Without vision, *good* things will keep us from achieving *great* things. Without vision, we are not directed but we become distracted.

People without clear vision are easily sidetracked and have a tendency to drift from one place to another with no spiritual, relational, financial, or moral compass. Consequently, their decisions, or lack of decisions, rob them of their destiny. In Ephesians 4:13, 14, Paul exhorted us believers to be a people of unity in the faith and of the knowledge of Jesus to become mature so that we are not tossed to and fro, carried from one doctrine to another. When we believers grow in maturity in the knowledge of Jesus Christ and in unity with one another, we receive God's vision for our lives. This vision provides true direction so we can make right decisions that will help us to fulfill our God-given dreams!

Essential Benefit #4:
Vision Gives You Purpose

The fourth essential benefit of having a hope-filled vision is purpose. When we believers understand the purpose of our vision, it will get us up every morning. If we don't show up for the day, something important will not happen. God's purpose in us is that big! The reason so many of us get up every morning to work a job is because we have gifts from God—our children—who are reliant on us to provide for them in every way. The reason so many of us pastors study the Word of God and prepare with diligence is because we have congregations and communities desperately waiting to hear a fresh word from God. We realize that we are not just working for ourselves; another person's life or ministry is depending on us! Suddenly our life matters.

We have purpose. Some of us are not parents or pastors, but our purpose in God is no less important. God values us. This is evident in the fact that we are all made individually and uniquely. God is entirely engaged in bringing about His perfect and mature will in our lives. His purpose is greater than we can think or imagine (1 Corinthians 2:9)!

Vision Driven by Hope

So what does vision have to do with hope? If we just have hope, we will shout, we will dance, we will have a few good weeks, and then we will have to face the reality that we have to walk out this hope. At times we must get up and face that devil and deal with opposition. We must work through setbacks and overcome failure because these are the realities of life. Having hope does not mean everything will be easy or it will just fall in place without encountering problems along the way.

Hold on to that hope which motivates
and drives your vision.

True hope is revealed when a person is facing life's difficulties and has every reason to give up, but cannot stop because there is something inside of them that is greater than what they are going through. They have the assurance that if they will hold on, not give up, and continue to move toward their goal, they will finish. Hope faces life's realities and continues undaunted.

True hope faces life's realities and continues undaunted.

The people of this world are searching to find a real church with real people in it who are practicing the Word of God. People who practice the Word of God are those who face the realities of life, go through them, and overcome them through the power of God that is in them. They have a vision greater than the moment in which they stand. Their hopeful future is ahead of them and they move toward it no matter the circumstance.

A hope-filled vision sees clearly, and although trying times and mistakes seem to blur the view, the vision is still there. God's hopeful vision ignites passion in us, motivates us, directs us and gives us purpose. Our vision may have been clouded by some tough places in life —divorce, loss of a loved one, setback at a job, loss of a job, loss of a home, cut in pay, broken contracts, and so many other things. But God's clear, hopeful vision inside of us would not let us quit. At times, we may have not known how we would put one foot in front of the next, but we did, and now we are moving even closer to the fulfillment of our destiny. The Holy Spirit is alive inside us believers, encouraging us: "Don't give up!" He says, "You can do it; you can make it. You can fulfill the dream and walk out the vision."

God is not finished with us yet!

A Vision Worth Pursuing

Thomas Edison, one of the greatest inventors in history and inventor of the incandescent light bulb, is one man who had a vision. Although he received 1,093 patents for his many important creations, he is also known as the inventor who experienced the most failures. For starters, Edison was nearly deaf and dropped out of school after the third grade. One of his teachers even commented that Edison was "too stupid to learn." How is that for encouragement? His invention of the light bulb only came after 10,000 failed attempts. In the eyes of most, he had failed many, many times and squandered a lot of money. However, Edison remarked that he had not failed 10,000 times, but rather discovered 10,000 ways that will not work![2] Those obstacles and failures did not stop him in pursuit of the success of his vision. They made him stronger because he had a vision that was worth pursuing. As a result, his inventions have had a tremendous impact upon all of our lives today.

Don't Give Up . . . I'm Not Finished With You Yet!

God too has a vision worth pursuing—**you** and **me**. In Jeremiah chapter 18, God told Jeremiah to go to the potter's house and watch. So he went and saw the potter making a vessel, but it was marred and

2 This story is part of the *Invention Mystery* series by author Paul Niemann. www.InventionMysteries.com

broken. He saw the potter take the vessel and remake it. God told Jeremiah that this is what He can do with his life. Speaking to Israel, what He can do with the nation. Today, God is speaking to us personally. His encouragement to us is that it may look like the situation we are in will never work out, but when He puts His hands to it, He can take what seems to have no hope, no possibility of making it, and He will reform and refashion it and bring the vision to its original purpose. In Jeremiah 18:6 He said, *"I will make a vessel fit for my use."*

Having vision is about God fulfilling His plan through us, His children, and in doing so, a watching world can see our loving, benevolent Heavenly Father. Ultimately when you and I come to the end of our lives, we will look back at our life and say we did it with the help of God. When obstacles and failures come our way, we must not give up. Instead, we must set our vision, keep the passion, motivation, direction, and purpose alive. We must stay the course and walk out our God-given, hope-filled vision, knowing that it is *He* who will complete the good work that He has begun in us (Philippians 1:6).

CHAPTER EIGHT
Hope ...
Nearer Means Seeing Clearer

Psalm 73 is a story, a song of remembering the will of God for our lives. One of David's worship directors by the name of Asaph was facing a dilemma. His world was dreadful because those who were living wickedly seemed to be getting away with their acts without consequence. His world was not unlike ours is today. In our world it seems that the bad guys are winning the lottery, the business wars, and the political offices. They seem to have all the money, success, fame, and happiness that anyone could ever dream of. What is worse, the good guys are having a tough time. Their lives are a mess. Their businesses are struggling. Instead of having more money than they need, there seems to be more "month" left at the end of their money. Their health is failing. Their kids are always sick or in trouble. One might question, why keep following God if suffering seems to be the daily price for the pursuit of God? In this chapter, we will take a look at Psalm 73, as Asaph recounted a litany of the ways of evil men, but in the end he provided a very clear solution to his problem. We will discover that if we want to see clearer we must move nearer to God.

If you want to see clearer, you must move nearer to God.

Ironically, Psalm 73 and its numerical counterpart Psalm 37 complement one another. They both deal with the heritage and blessings of the righteous, as well as the calamity of the wicked. In Psalm 73 Asaph talked about his personal life, and in Psalm 37 David addressed his military men, because their perception of the matter was causing them to feel defeated. Their view literally caused them to lose hope and have the mindset, "What is the use? Why even try?" Just like David's men, if we look at what is going on around us, we will lose hope. We must redirect our vision and understand that seeing clearly is only going to happen when we draw nearer to God.

Don't Get Yourself in a "WAD"

Here we believers are, trucking along in life and doing just fine. Our eyes are on God and we are doing what we believe we should do. Then, all of the sudden, the bad guys catch our attention. They are doing all the wrong things and getting away with it! It does not seem fair. Now life doesn't look so good and everything seems to be going the wrong way for us. We have just gotten ourselves in a wad. How did that happen? In this scenario we began watching the ways of the wicked, then we became entangled in the cares of life and lost our perspective; in turn, wc lost hope. When we have a right perspective, we see God. We have hope because we know if God is *for* us, who in the world can be *against* us? Let's examine the snares in which Asaph found himself in Psalm 73 and discuss the three wrong ways of thinking that can cause us to get in a wad, using the acrostic for the word WAD.

Wrong Way of Thinking #1:
Want What Others Seem to Have

The first way to get into a wad is by *wanting* what others seem to have. Asaph remarked in Psalm 73:1-3,

> God is good to Israel, to such as are pure in heart. But as for me, my feet had almost stumbled; my steps had nearly slipped. For I was envious of the boastful, when I saw the prosperity of the wicked.

Asaph simply said that he almost fell when he took his eyes off of where they should be. He began looking at what was going on around him and the seeming prosperity of the wicked and almost fell. Sometimes, we believers are so busy looking at everyone else, what they have, and what they are doing that we find ourselves losing our joy and hope. We then become frustrated, angry, jealous, and envious. Instead, we must continue looking through our own window of hope.

Remember Rahab's window to which she secured the scarlet cord, her hope? She peered out her window and saw God. If we view life from others' perspectives of greed, lust, and covetousness, then we will not see life from God's window of hope and we get ourselves into a wad. When we put our hope in other *things* we misplace our hope. Therefore, we think we are only valuable when we have things. It is only when we get our eyes back on God that situations and circumstances make sense and become clear. Focusing our gaze on God and gaining His understanding brings us clarity.

Before we try to keep up with what our neighbor has or where they are going, we had better find out what their goal is, what their vision is about. On the surface it may look like they are a complete success, but because they do not have a God-vision, their life is ultimately leading them away from God. In Psalm 73:2-3, Asaph recognized that he almost slipped and fell into the deception of living in compromise by *looking* at the prosperity of the wicked. When we *look* at and envy the prosperity of the wicked, we get into trouble. Taking long, envious looks at what we think we see, wanting it, lusting for it, playing with it in our minds, and imagining we have it, are good first steps for poor visibility that weakens our hope.

Wrong Way of Thinking #2:
Assume the Bad Guys are Getting Away with Everything

The second way to get into a wad is *assume* the bad guys are getting away with everything. Asaph continued by saying,

> *For there are no pangs in their death, but their strength is firm. They are not in trouble as other men, nor are they plagued like other men . . . Their eyes bulge with abundance; they have more than heart could wish. They scoff and speak wickedly concerning oppression; they speak loftily . . . And they say, "How does God know? And is there knowledge in the Most High?" Behold, these are the ungodly, who are always at ease; they increase in riches . . . When I thought how to understand this, it was too painful for me.* (Psalm 73:4-5, 7-8, 11-12, 16)

The ungodly people Asaph referred to in this passage were the Israelites who were supposed to be in covenant with God, who mocked Him. Asaph was not writing about the reprobates who worshipped carved images. In all of this, it seemed as though God was not doing one cotton-picking thing about it! Have you ever secretly wanted God to zap someone you knew was a rascal, who was getting away with it? Everyone is singing their praises and you want to spill all the beans! The ungodly were doing these things and seeming to get away with it. It is just not fair! The psalmist seemed to be the victim of this type of thinking. We must not get caught up in this thinking trap. Rather, we must have God's perspective.

Short-term Thinking is a Dead End. According to verse 12, Asaph saw the wealth and apparent (temporary) success of the wicked and, as a result, felt miserable. He was trying to focus on God's plan for his life, one day at a time, but he was distracted and did not have a clear understanding of what was taking place around him. I believe

Asaph felt overwhelmed because he viewed life with short-term think-ing. This type of thinking lacks the understanding of the plan of God.

Anger and Passion don't Mix. I believe Asaph was angry about what he saw. Anger can arise when we take our eyes off God's plan. It may not be an outward show of anger, but anger is there. We begin to ask the question, "How can people live wickedly and not get what is com-ing to them; all the while I am living right and struggling with life?"

Let's consider gasoline. It is great for fuel and power, but if stored in the wrong place, it becomes dangerous. Gasoline stored in a house, next to the furnace, will explode! Anger can be likened to gasoline, and our passion or vision can be likened to the furnace. When we allow anger to rise up and sit next to our passion, it can blow up inside us. We will end up saying or doing the something we will regret because we assume the bad guys are escaping justice, and we think God is not looking. Proverbs 24:20 says, "*Do not fret because of evil men or be envi-ous of the wicked, for the evil man has no future hope, and the lamp of the wicked will be snuffed out*" (NIV). God is looking.

Assumptions Lead to Hopelessness. It is very important that we don't assume the wicked are prospering in their ways. We can be side-tracked from hope when we assume that others are successful while doing and acting wrongly. Asaph almost fell because he was watching the wicked instead of God. This trap is a very slippery slope. If we take our eyes off of God, our assumptions will drag us down, rob us of our joy, and steal our hope and peace.

Instead of assuming the wicked are flourishing in their ways, we should read God's Word and find out what He says about the wicked, and more importantly, what God says about us. We should make the decision to believe His Word and stop assuming the lies of our enemy. Instead of giving anger a place in our heart, we should let God's hope arise within us. We need to become sensitive to the prompting of the Holy Spirit when we find ourselves in these circumstances. We never know when God may want to give us the opportunity to speak a word of love, acceptance, and forgiveness to a brother or sister in Christ that will help them see the error of their ways and bring hope and clarity to their personal window.

Wrong Way of Thinking #3:
Downplay the Decision to Follow and Trust God

The third way to get into a wad is *downplay* the decision we made to follow and trust God. I believe most of us Christians deal with this wrong way of thinking when we a trying to live right. It seems that everywhere we look people are acting, talking, and living the wrong way and seem to be thriving, and all the while, we are doing our best to walk out all that God has called us to do without seeming to make much progress. It is in this type of thinking that we question our decision to follow and trust God. Is His plan really the best plan? In Psalm 73:13-15, Asaph responded to all he had seen:

> *Surely I have cleansed my heart in vain, and washed my hands in innocence. For all day long I've been plagued, and chastened every morning. If I had said, 'I will speak thus,' behold, I would have been untrue to the generation of your children.*

This is my interpretation of the psalmist's viewpoint: "I feel like a fool for following God, for being ethical, and for being kind. In vain I have kept my mind pure and I have stayed clean. Instead, my co-workers cut shady deals, make tons of money, party every night, sleep around, and fulfill every demented dream they ever had. They sleep in on Sunday and spend Wednesday nights down at the bar and everything is going their way. They laugh at my church affiliation, calling me crazy and nuts for spending my time there and talking about God and His goodness. Even though I do and say the right things, I don't seem to have their success. I feel like a fool for following and trusting God!"

Maybe that is an exaggeration, but I believe this frame of mind is how so many Christians stumble. When we espouse this wrong type of thinking, we end up hedging our relationship with the One who created us. Christians often do not trust God as we should because so many of us have tried trusting Him before and it did not work out like we thought it was supposed to work out. When things don't work out like we want them to, we pull back in our relationship with God and live in fear and frustration. Living this way keeps us at a distance from Him and from the answers He wants to give. When we are detached from God by wishing for someone else's life, we end up feeling like a fool with poor vision and diminished hope.

Let's not get ourselves in a "WAD" by wanting what we think others have, assuming the bad guys are getting away with their evil schemes, and downplaying our decision to follow and trust God. Instead, let us move ever closer to God, the One who made all, sees all, and knows all. It is Him we believers should desire to see. It is His perspective we need in order to walk in the hope He promised us.

CHAPTER NINE
Hope ...
Take a Closer Look and See

After expressing his frustration and anger about the ways of the wicked and the seeming injustice of the righteous in Psalm 73, Asaph finally uncovered the mystery to handling these hardships: if you want to see God clearer, simply step nearer to Him. Asaph discovered that gazing upon the wicked was getting him nowhere and found the answer to his problems was in seeing God, and gaining His viewpoint. Based on Asaph's discovery, let's examine three ways to improve our vision and strengthen our hope using an acrostic for the word SEE.

If you want to see God clearer,
simply step nearer to Him.

Way #1 to Improve Vision and Strengthen Hope:
<u>S</u>tep Closer to God

The first way to have a clearer, hopeful vision is to simply step closer to God. In Psalm 73:16 Asaph expressed, *"When I thought how to understand this, it was too painful for me."* What I love about Asaph is that he didn't stop in his frustration, content to be angry and in pain, and feeling sorry for himself. He continued in verse 17, *"Until I went into the sanctuary of God; then I understood their end."* What does that mean? It means when we go to stand before God and be near to Him, we can see and understand the truth. We then know the end of the matter. As Paul Harvey might say, "And that is ... the rest of the story."

It is good for me to draw near to God because I can know the rest of the story. Asaph went on to say in verse 28, *"But it is good for me to draw near to God; I have put my trust in the Lord God, that I may declare all of your works."*

Stepping closer to God sounds rather simple, but the truth of the matter is most of us are following Him from a distance. We are afraid of getting too close because we might have to give up something we value or stop doing something we want to continue. So we follow God at a distance, keeping Him near enough to call on Him when life gets crazy. Otherwise, we don't bother Him until we need Him. If we want to have a clearer vision, we must step closer to the Lord.

Stepping Closer is a Choice. Stepping closer to God is a choice. We must choose it everyday. So many of us Christians want to come down to the altar in church, cry a bunch of tears, have God touch us, and feel His presence. But if tomorrow morning we get up and do not *feel* the same way, we think God has left. He has not left just because our "feeler" has gone out. God may be waiting to see how we will respond to what we perceive as His absence. Instead, we should draw near to Him with all humility, submitting our lives to Him. When we do this, He promises to draw near to us (James 4:8). He desires fellowship and companionship with us. He is waiting.

He also promised in Deuteronomy 4:29, *"Seek Me and you will find Me."* In Jeremiah 33:3 He encouraged, *"Call to Me, and I will answer you."* We must take that first step every day. When we seek Him, He will position Himself for us to find Him. When we call to Him and communicate with Him, He will answer. To gain the right perspective and to see clearly we must first step closer to God. When we are closer to God we have hope because we see God's potential for our lives.

If we believers in Jesus Christ will look out of our spiritual windows, we will see our hope, the good future God has designed for us. If we will walk with Him and stay in covenant with Him, He will protect and bless us. He will do everything His Word promises! That is hope!

What is the Position of My Heart? The word *heart* is mentioned six times in Psalm 73 (vv. 1, 7, 13, 21, 26). For Christians this is not just an important issue, it is the *key* issue. The apex of Christian faith is not purity in religion, doctrine, attendance and appearance, but purity of heart, genuine motive brought about only by the heart-changing work of Jesus Christ. Purity of heart speaks about relationship with God. We are either building a good relationship or we are building a bad one, and it is our choice. Let's choose to step closer to God and build a relationship with Him that reveals a heart motivated by love.

The psalmist Asaph was deeply in love with the Lord (Psalm 73:25). When we fall in love with God we gain His perspective, and, consequently, every temporal thing on this earth grows strangely dim. It is then that our present life and circumstances become to us a poor copy, a mutilated image, and a pale theology of the true life we have in Christ.

Do you want to win the war with envy, materialism, gossip, a judgmental attitude, and have a clearer vision and stronger hope? Come nearer to Him! You can step near to God in many ways; through a simple prayer, changing of a bad habit, or maybe a commitment to opening your Bible with a predisposition to listen, learn, and live. No matter what it is that you need, your first step is toward God.

Way #2 to Improve Vision and Strengthen Hope: Evaluate the Future

The second way to have a clearer, hopeful vision is to evaluate the future. Evaluate the futures of two people, the wicked and the God-follower. What happens to the wicked? Asaph revealed the answer in

Psalm 73:17-18, *"Until I went into the sanctuary of God; then I under-stood their end. Surely You set them in slippery places."* It may look like the wicked are cutting the shady deals and getting away with it right now, but God has set them on a slippery slope. If they don't wake up and realize what they are doing, they will slide into judgment. There is a heaven and there is a hell, and both are for eternity. Every person on earth makes a choice that determines the outcome of their eternal future. Some may believe that a loving God would not send anyone to hell. God is not *sending* anyone there. Rather, they are making the *choice* to go there. They are choosing not to cooperate with the prin-ciples of God, not to submit their life to the Lord by accepting Jesus Christ as their Savior and Redeemer. Asaph almost fell down that slip-pery slope himself. In verse 27, he went on to say, *"For indeed, those who are far from You shall perish; You have destroyed all those who desert You."* Destruction is the future for the wicked.

In contrast, the future of the God-follower is full of hope, one that is based on God's promises in and through Christ Jesus. It does not mean we believers are perfect or that we have everything worked out. It just means that we know who we are connected to, that we have accepted Jesus Christ as Lord and Savior. If not, we will spend eterni-ty apart from God. Hell is worse than we can imagine and heaven is far better than we can imagine.

Asaph encouraged himself in the Lord in verses 23-26:

Nevertheless I'm continually with You; You hold me by my right hand. You guide me with your counsel, and afterward receive me to glory. Whom have I in heaven but You? And there is none upon earth that I desire besides You. My flesh and my heart fail; but God is the strength of my heart and my portion forever.

God will bless and take care of us, the ones who follow Him. Our vision will be different because our future will be greater. What God has in store for us will far outweigh our present circumstances.

When our eyes are on the incomparable future God has planned for us, we cannot help but choose life in Jesus Christ. It is like the story, found in John 6:60-68, where Jesus had preached a difficult Word for the people to receive and many of them went away from Him, rejecting the truth. After this He turned to His disciples in verse 67 and asked, *"Are you going to leave me too?"* Peter replied in verse 68, *"Lord, where can we go? Because You have the words to eternal life"* (NIV). We believers must also evaluate our future, choose to improve our vision, and strengthen our hope. When we get our eyes back on the Lord everything will be okay.

Way #3 to Improve Vision and Strengthen Hope: Enjoy Your Relationship with God

The third way to have a clearer, hopeful vision is to simply enjoy our relationship with God. When we love someone we enjoy being around them. We find reasons and take opportunities to be with them. By the way some of us conduct our relationship with God it seems that we just don't like Him because we find reasons *not* to fellowship with Him. We find excuses *not* to be near Him. If we would begin to *enjoy* our relationship with God, we would see so clearly.

God loves us! He is *for* us and not *against* us. He knows everything about us, all that we have ever done, are doing, and will ever do, and yet He still invites us to come to Him. He is not like most of us who tend to scrutinize each other's actions, where if we don't measure up, we won't be accepted. God knows everything about us and still He invites us to come. He loves, accepts, and forgives us just the way we are. That is amazing! Why wouldn't we want to enjoy a relationship with God?

Position Yourself to Get the Best Vantage Point. It makes sense for a photographer to position himself and the lens of his camera to get just the right angle and lighting for the perfect snapshot. Similarly, we believers must align our hearts and minds with God's viewpoint and in light of His Word in order to have clearer vision. We must position ourselves to gain the best vantage point for seeing our destiny. Sometimes seeing something from one perspective does not afford the best outlook, but if we change positions, the view can be spectacular. We need to be willing to re-direct our focus to maximize the vision God has for us.

I believe the reason so many people in our culture and society have lost hope is because they are looking everywhere except to God for direction. They put all their stock into what Hollywood says about them and what Wall Street says about their situation. They believe that the government and the right person in the political office can solve all their problems, when in reality, those presiding in political positions are just men and women with faults and shortcomings just like the rest of us.

We Christians are not immune to comparing ourselves with others. We get our focus off of God when we look at another person's life, where we they are, what they have, or where they are going, and evaluate ourselves to them. In doing this, we essentially place them in position that God desires to have in our life. We make them our idol, and subsequently, we want their gifts, wealth, and favor, instead of desiring God and His perfect plan for our lives. By redirecting our vision toward God, we have the right perspective to live in hope.

The song of Psalm 73 teaches us that when we look at life's circumstances we lose true sight. What I love about the psalmist Asaph is that he saw what was happening around him but he caught himself before he fell into the trap that was prepared for the wicked. Similarly, we believers will see evil all around us, but we do not have to allow it to entangle or distract us. In the light of God's vantage point, we can see the ways of the wicked for what they truly are and understand that these times in which we live will not last forever. Our future hope is in God!

Clear Vision is Hope!

Hope is the confident expectation of a desired future state. *Hope* is what God has for us. *Vision* is looking forward with *hope* toward the expected promises of God. So **clear vision is just seeing what God is saying about us—this is hope!** God is talking. Are we listening? God is declaring our future. Can we see it? If we are looking out the window of hope, the scarlet cord, the *tiqvah*, assures that we have a good future, because God is going before us.

Vision is simply seeing what God is saying.

The reality is that, in life, we will encounter some tough places. The walls around us are going to shake, but if we stay in covenant like Rahab did, although they fall on our right and left, the destruction will not come near us (Psalm 91:7). Until God is finished with us, we are not going anywhere. Instead, we should take a closer look and "SEE" what we have not seen before, by stepping nearer to God, evaluating our future in Him, and then sitting back to enjoy the journey. Enjoy the relationship with God and maintain hope.

If you have been seeking to have clearer vision, a steadfast hope, and a closer relationship with God in the midst of your circumstances, I invite you to pray this prayer, right where you are:

> *God, here is my life. You know everything about me. You see my end from my beginning, my beginning from my end. You already know every choice, every decision that I'm going to make. Lord, I ask You in this moment in time to help me to see correctly. Help*

me Father to step closer to You. Help me, God to have a true evaluation of how this is all going to end up. Lord, I want to enjoy You. God, I am going to have a long journey and I want the journey to be enjoyable. I want to build a relationship with You, in Jesus' Name, amen.

CHAPTER TEN
Hope ...
Staring Down Trouble

Do you sometimes feel like you are living under Murphy's Law? Murphy's Law states whatever *can* go wrong *will* go wrong. I would like to attach my little addendum to it—not only will it go wrong, but it will usually go wrong over and over again. Murphy's Law also implies that if the bottom falls out, you can rest assured that the walls are going to fall in on you too.

Now, we all have difficult days. They are not uncommon to any of us. We all have moments in our life when we absolutely do not know how we are going to make it. I would love to be able to say that, when we have hope, everything is going to be easy from then on. Hope has to be more than a "sunny day" experience, more than just something we feel when we can finally see it is going to work out okay. Hope has to be a substance inside of us, the soil in which faith is sown, our foundation. It has to be there in the good times and the bad times. Hope must play a greater role in our lives now than it has in our past. There will be difficult days ahead of us, but for the child of God they need not be fatal or destructive days. They can be days lined with possibility if we understand how to look at them correctly, go through them, and learn what God wants us to learn. Hope has the ability to see trouble and to be able to know what to do with it.

Hope has the ability to see trouble and know what to do with it.

In this chapter we will discuss and define days of trouble, explore their purpose in our lives, and in taking with us their experiences, look with hope-filled eyes beyond today and into our future. We will learn the keys to turning our tests and trials into triumph! Believe it or not, days of trouble not only add value to our lives, but are essential for the shaping of our destinies in God!

Count It All Joy When You Face Trouble!

The Apostle James wrote to the 12 tribes of Israel, the believing Jews who became Christians, and said, *"James, a bondservant of God, of the Lord Jesus Christ to the twelve tribes which are scattered abroad, greetings. My brethren, count it all joy . . . "* (James 1:1-5). He did not waste any time. I like this about James' writings. You never have to wonder where he stood on an issue. He said what he meant and it is clear:

> *Count it all joy when you fall into various [**different types or many**] trials [**tests**], knowing that the testing of your faith produces patience. But let patience have its perfect work, that you may be perfect and complete, lacking nothing. If any of you lacks wisdom, let him ask of God, who gives to all liberally and without reproach, and it will be given to him.*

At the very beginning of his letter, James wanted to help the new Christians understand why they are experiencing difficult days. Notice that he addressed this letter to the twelve tribes of Israel that were scattered. James wrote this letter at a time early in the Christian faith, and at that time, Christianity was viewed by the watching world as just another phase of Judaism, even though all Jews—orthodox and Christian—recognized the difference. The Christian Jews embraced their Judaic heritage but also adopted belief in Jesus Christ as the Son of God, the fulfillment of the law, while the orthodox Jews rejected Jesus Christ as the Messiah. James wrote to those people who were following Christ, but were going through tough times. Their businesses were being boycotted, their children were being attacked, they were being talked about in the marketplace, and they were seen as outcasts in their communities because they believed in Jesus Christ. Not only were the orthodox Jews looking down on them, but now Rome was casting a suspicious eye on them because they practiced communion and professed the words of Jesus concerning eating His flesh and drinking His blood (John 6:58). These early Christians experienced many persecutions.

During the time of the first and second century Church, life as a Christian was extremely tough. It cost you. Often times, it cost your life and the life of your family or business. Today, we talk about blessing, victory, and all these wonderful things. We, the Church in America, have so westernized the Gospel that we don't understand the purpose or the reason why we experience some of the trouble we experience. Sometimes the difficulties we Christians face are not brought on because we are bad or because we have sinned. Sometimes, troubles come because we are Christians.

---

*Having and living in hope is not
a denial of our present circumstances,
but it is standing and facing them
with a God-given vision.*

I believe that the Apostle James wanted to impart to those suffering Christians a measure of hope, clarity, and purpose. It was to this group of believers that this loving pastor wanted to give insight and bring understanding that would make sense out of their difficult dilemma. The hope he offered to them then is the same hope God is offering us today. Remember, hope is the confident expectation of a desired future condition. Having and living in hope is not a denial of our present circumstances, but it is standing and facing them with a God-given vision.

Defining Days of Trouble: Did I Bring This On Myself?

In order for us to maintain hope during these difficult days, we must understand that days of trouble can come to us by one of two ways: self or sin-made troubles, or the cares of life. The trials, afflictions, or tests James referred to in James chapter one are not self or sin-made messes. He was not referring to the problems that we bring on ourselves by the decisions that we make, nor was he talking about the repercussions of the sins we have committed—like the time when you broke the law going 95 miles-per-hour in a 35 miles-per-hour zone, and the cop pulls you over and drags your carcass down to the pokey and puts you in there! No, you did that. James was not talking about the difficult time you are having because you got caught cheating on a test.

---

*God sees something greater in you
than you see in yourself!*

James was also not talking about something you have done that God has addressed as morally or sexually wrong. James made it clear in verse 13 that *"God cannot be tempted by evil, nor does He Himself tempt anyone."* Let me just say that God is not placing in front of you opportunities for you to fail in the area of morality. That is the devil tempting you! Guard your heart and step closer to God so you can discern the right choices to make.

We must also remember that when we do make wrong choices and fall into sin, if we will turn to God, He is there to pick us up. Because of the awesome power of His grace God will even use our dumb choices to bring us good and teach us about His unconditional love. I love this about God! He will make use of our sin and the mess that we made. 1 John 1:9 promises that if we "*confess our sins, He is faithful and just to forgive us our sins and to cleanse us from all unrighteousness.*" That sin which should be destroying us, disqualifying us or wiping us out, God will use to bring about our good and His glory. He sees something greater in us than we even see in ourselves. He did not cause this trouble to happen, but He loves us too much to leave us there, so He is going to help us through our mess. Now, there is hope!

Defining Days of Trouble:
Troubles Brought on by the Cares of Life

When James exhorted believers to, "*Count it all joy when you fall into various [**different types or many**] trials [**tests**]*" in James 1:2, he was referring to the trials, those days of trouble which were allowed entrance into the lives of the Christian believers. Even when we do all that we know to do right, the cares of life are there. Notice that James did not say "if" trials or tests come, instead, he said *"when,"* because they are coming, no matter our place in life.

So You Had a Bad Day

In his song *Bad Day,* Daniel Powter describes what most of us experience to be a stream of unfortunate circumstances:

> *They tell me your blue skies fade to gray*
> *They tell me your passion's gone away*
> *and 'I don't need no carryin on'*

. . . You stand in line just to hit a new low
You're faking a smile with the coffee you go

You tell me your life's been way off line
You're falling to pieces every time

. . . Because you had a bad day.[1]

The truth is every single one of us faces difficult days, regardless of where we are from and all the things that we have attempted to do correctly. In fact, a lot of times the difficulties we face have nothing to do with anything we have done or not done, as far as a choice that would necessarily have a negative consequence.

The passage of scripture in James 1:2 correlates to the times when you are living a good life, walking out the Christian faith, making every effort to do the right thing, and trouble finds you. Maybe you have tried to be the best wife or husband you could be to your spouse. You were faithful to them, loved them, and did everything you knew to do. You know you were not perfect, but you did your best to be what they needed, only to find out that they were involved in a relationship outside your marriage.

Maybe you are having a tough time because you have a mean, obnoxious neighbor who, no matter how hard you try to get along with them and try to build a relationship with them, they are just unkind and making life difficult for you. Maybe you were working diligently at your job, preparing to receive a promotion that was headed your way. You met the criteria, worked hard and did everything that was asked of you, but for some reason you got passed over for someone else. Not only that, but you know the person they promoted had been a slacker and cut corners. Yet, they were promoted. They got the raise and you didn't.

---

1 "Bad Day," Daniel Powter. *Daniel Powter* CD. Warner Brothers, 2005.

Maybe you chose to prefer and bless someone, but instead of them appreciating the blessing, they turned and slandered you. Maybe you worked diligently to operate your company with wisdom and integrity, but because a deal fell through, your business went bankrupt. Maybe you received a phone call out of nowhere with terminal news that said, "You know that lump I told you not to concern yourself with? You need to come back in. We have to talk." Maybe you lost a loved one unexpectedly. Have you faced life that way?

You may even be asking God, "Why? Why me? Why this? Why this now? What have I done to get this? How is any good going to come out of this?" All been there, haven't we? Some of you are there now. Some of you are going there. Some of you are coming out of there. "There" has been somewhere all of us have gone to at some time or another. We all have to face these days, these moments in our lives.

Our hope in the midst of these days is that God knows these troubles, trials, and tests are coming and He has a plan for them. As a matter of fact, the Apostle Peter in 1 Peter 4:12-13a encouraged us to not be surprised upon their arrival when he said, *"do not think it strange concerning the fiery trial which is to try you, as though some strange thing happened to you; but rejoice . . ."* Troubles are going to happen, but rejoice! Bad days are not a possibility, but a reality of what we all face. I do not believe God is just allowing these troubles to come to us for no good reason. Rather, He wants us to see and understand who we are through them.

Purpose of Difficult Days: Finding the Good in the Bad

Not only do we need to understand that difficult days are going to come, we must find out what difficult days do, what is their purpose in our lives. Hope says to our hearts that there must be some good even in the midst of the bad. James 1:3-4 states, *"knowing that the testing of your faith produces patience **[endurance, perseverance]**. But let patience have its perfect work, that you may be perfect and complete, lacking nothing."* It is really simple. When you are going through difficult days with faith and hope believing, God's purposes will begin to happen in your life.

Hope says to our hearts that there must be some good even in the midst of the bad!

God's Purpose #1:
Tests Make You Strong

Allow me to give you *my* translation of James 1:4 —*"So let patience—perseverance—let it grow! And don't try to squirm out of your problems."* Let's be honest; facing difficulty, troubles, trials, and tests are not our first choice in life. So many times, during these tests, the tendency is to cut and run, to escape the trial. Yet when we face them and allow God to work in us through them, we become strong. When we come *through* our test, we will be stronger. The Greek word for patience, perseverance literally means *to stay under.* I love watching the barbell power-lifters in the Olympics. For these power lifters to be successful they have to lift the weight, hold it up, and stay under it for a measured time, not forever, but for an appointed time. Why? To reveal their strength. The endurance of their test proves their strength. Tests, trials, and adversity come, but instead of them crushing us, for the length of time that it is necessary, we stand and are made strong.

Tests produce the strength we need to endure difficulty when everyone else is jumping ship.

Difficult days are often God's way of making us into what we truly want to be—strong, spirit-filled power-lifters for the kingdom of God. It is that strength we need to be able to endure difficulty when everyone else is quitting and jumping ship. It is the strength to stand and not crumble or fall under the weight. Some of the Olympic athletes do fall, but they get right back into training because they refuse to believe that they cannot stand. I love that type of character! If we can only succeed and walk with God when we do it perfectly every single time, none of us will make it because we will all find our limits. When every person finds his limit, he has to make up in his heart and mind, "Am I going to let the limit stop me, or am I going to be willing to condition myself, so I can be able to stand under this pressure? I will not be beat!"

I want to clarify something here. God is not in the business of killing your family, destroying your business or anything else to somehow try to mature you. Instead, He knows when difficulty is going to come and He uses what the enemy meant for evil. So stay the course and stand under the temporary pressure with the confident expectation that God will produce in you strength that you did not have before!

God's Purpose #2:
Tests Make You Grow and Advance

Difficulties make us strong, but they also help us grow and advance in all that God has for us to do. Patience and perseverance has a work to do. Trials examine to help us find the weak parts of our armor so that we can grow in that area and become a more useful vessel to God. In James 1:4, the Apostle James described the process of endurance through trials in order that patience and perseverance be worked out in us, and encouraged us not to stop short of becoming perfect. Did he say "perfect?" Perfection, in this sense, does not refer to being sinless. Rather, it means to be fully developed or mature. So, if God says we can become perfect, that means we have some growing to do! I don't know about you, but I want to be complete and not lacking. I want my faith and my life to be mature, to be all that God has called me to be. We believers must be willing to endure some tests in order for *His* perfection to be worked out in us.

We may need to consider that God may not be testing us to remove something from us, but rather, He may want to begin something new in our lives. The test in which we find ourselves may just be a set up by God to launch us into a new spiritual dimension of life in Him. Although the place we are in may seem scary, fear does not have to grip us. 1 John 4:18 says, *"perfect love casts out fear."* Maybe God is allowing us to be positioned in what we see as a fearful place or an impossible situation, only to show us that He will take care of us, that His love is being perfected in us.

Maybe the test God has prepared for us is whether or not we can handle a blessing, to determine if we are trustworthy to receive more. God may be allowing the test because He has something greater in store for us. Just like being tested at the end of the school year to see if we really know the material in order to move on to the next grade, before we advance to the next level God has for us, we have to pass the test!

God's Purpose #3:
Tests Reveal the *Real* You

I am reminded of the story about the great South Dakota masterpiece Mount Rushmore. On the side of the mountain is a monumental carving of four American presidents: George Washington, Thomas Jefferson, Abraham Lincoln and Theodore Roosevelt. When asked how he produced this amazing work, Gutzon Borglum, lead architect and sculptor on the project said, "Those figures were there for 40 million years. All I had to do was dynamite 400,000 tons of granite to bring them into view." There are many things keeping the real you, your strength and your character, from being viewed. God is just removing those things so the real you can be seen by others. God incarnate, Jesus Christ, is *in* you, and He is the hope of glory (Colossians 1:27). Yes, Christ, *your hope* lives *in* you! This is what I call "incarnational" Christianity—Christ *in* us and *through* us to the world.

The *real* you, the mighty man or woman of faith and keeper of hope, the one who is strong, tenacious, and determined, who stands under the pressure and will not give up, that *real* you is just hidden behind some attitudes and actions in your life. God loves you too much not to bring the real you out, because when He made you, He made you in His image. You may have been marred by life's difficulties, you may have been abused or abandoned, and you may have had the odds stacked against you, but God is going to cut away all of that mess to reveal the real you. All you need to do is put the scalpel of the Word of God to your life and cut away what is not like Him. Allow Him to dynamite out those strongholds that have been holding you down and let the real you come shining forth! That is why you have hope, because you are becoming like Him! Will the *real* you please stand up?

Tests not only reveal to yourself what you are made of, but they also show who you are to a watching world. When you face difficulty, know that someone is always watching you, waiting to see how you will respond. Sometimes the tests come in order to show your integrity to a co-worker, or to reveal your faith in God for healing your body to someone who needs a miracle. The test may be what kind of attitude you are going to have *when* you are tested! Anyway you slice it, what is on the inside of you will be revealed in a test!

When you buy clothing or appliances there is usually a tag on the inside that reads, "Inspected by . . . " You, too, should have an "Inspected by" tag in your life, where the Inspector (God) looked at you and said, "Real Deal. They have got the goods. When you push the wash cycle, they know how to wash. When you push the rinse cycle, they know how to get it clean. They are the Real Deal!" When the world looks at you they should see that you are made out of the cloth that the advertisement says you are, "100% Child of God," then they will see and want the hope that is inside of you!

Hope Says "Trouble? Bring It On!"

Many Christians understand hope as always having sunny days, singing about sunshine and the birds chirping. It is kind of like joy, anyone can have joy when circumstances are right. The real test of joy, the real test of faith, and the real test of hope is when things are not going well and the unexpected and the seemingly undeserved happens. We all experience these times in our life. It is our reaction to them that really reveals whether we are living in faith with hope believing or whether we are circumstantial Christians.

When trouble continues to knock at the door of the lives of some Christians, their response is one of hopelessness. They conclude that because they have experienced so much trouble that this is just the way life is and it is never going to change. They have lived this way for so long that they are numb to the pain and resolve to believe that God cannot and will not change their circumstances. Pain for extended periods of time produces numbness, which is likened to deadness. So many people have suffered greatly in life and have allowed the troubles and cares of life to deaden them to hope, the expectation of living in the promises of God. In John 10:10, Jesus revealed the truth by saying, *"The thief does not come except to steal, and to kill, and to destroy. I have come that they may have life, and that they may have it more abun-*

dantly." This being true, God must have a plan and a purpose for the troubles we face, and His plan is *not* that they destroy us, but that we have life *abundantly*—excessive, overflowing, and more than enough! Many times, we parents desire good things for our children, even though we may not always have the means to provide for them. God not only *desires* for us to live in His fullness, but has actually *provided* the way for us to have it. Through the sacrifice of His Son, Jesus Christ, we have been given all that we need to live this life with hope.

No matter the type of adversity, self or sin-made trouble or trouble brought on by the cares of life, we can stand up and stare it down, knowing that our God, the Almighty One has a plan to make us strong, help us to grow and advance, so that the *real* us, the believers in Jesus Christ, can be revealed to a watching, love-sick-for-God world. Trouble doesn't know it, but it is helping to make us into vessels of hope for this world!

CLOSING
Hope ... Hold Out for Your Promised Expectation

As we come to the close of our journey to a life of hope, we have discovered some powerful truths that will sustain us in the years to come. 1 Corinthians 2:9 promises, *"Eye has not seen, nor ear heard, nor have entered into the heart of man the things which God has prepared for those who love Him."* Therefore, as we love God with all of our heart, soul, and strength, we meet the requirements for God's promise of hope. We can grab hold of this hope and claim His promises personally. Hope is ours to own and live, no matter our circumstance.

I love what God said to unrepentant Israel through His prophet Jeremiah, *"For I know the thoughts that I think toward you, says the LORD, thoughts of peace and not of evil, to give you a future and a hope"* (Jeremiah 29:11). The word hope there has the same meaning as *tiqvah,* the rope or cord, the lifeline. We can never forget the scarlet cord that is hanging out the window of our life. We should lift up our head, gaze in the right direction, and know that God is with us. The tests we experience are not meant to break, destroy, hurt, or harm us. They are to build the character of God in us and reveal that character to the world.

Even though we Christians sometimes want to escape from the tests and trials in our lives, they have been designed by God to build endurance in us. The Prophet Isaiah, in Isaiah 43:1-2 said, *"But now thus says the LORD who created you, and He formed you, 'O Jacob, O Israel, fear not for I have redeemed you. I have called you by your name. You are Mine.'"*This truth brings such comfort. He continued, *"When you pass through the waters,"* not "bridge *over* troubled waters," but *"when* you pass **through** the waters, I will be with you; and through the rivers, they shall not overflow you" [emphasis added]. In other words, when we walk through the fire of a trial, just like the three Hebrew boys did in Daniel 3:19-25, God will be with us. The fiery test will not burn or scorch us. We must also remember that tests are not meant to last forever. Our hope in God and His presence with us in the fire will sustain us, and we will emerge unharmed and even stronger because of it.

We all experience pressure. For some of us, the pressure is greater than it is for others. The question is, will the pressure push us *to* God or will it push us *from* God? It is our choice. Let's choose to draw near to Him, hold on to the *scarlet cord,* and experience the *door of hope, Jesus,* whom God has placed right in the midst of our trouble! The Apostle Peter encouraged believers in 1 Peter 1:3-9, 13 when he said,

> *Praise be to God and Father of our Lord Jesus Christ! In His great mercy He has given us new birth into a living* **hope** *through the resurrection of Jesus Christ from the dead, and into an inheritance that can never perish, spoil or fade—kept in heaven for you, who through faith are shielded by God's power until the coming of the salvation that is ready to be revealed in the last time. In this you greatly rejoice, though now for a little while you may have had to suffer grief in all kinds of trials. These have come so that your faith—of greater worth than gold, which perishes even though refined by fire—may be proved genuine and may result in praise, glory and honor when Jesus Christ is revealed. Though you have not seen Him, you love Him; and even though you do not see Him now, you believe in Him and are filled with an inexpressible and glorious joy, for you are receiving the goal of your faith, the salvation of your souls . . . Therefore, prepare your minds for action; be self-controlled; set your* **hope** *fully on the grace to be given you when Jesus Christ is revealed* [emphasis added].

In spite of what you see, in spite of what life is, if you hold onto your hope in Jesus Christ, you have the promise that you will receive your future expectation in Him. Remember the working definition of hope: hope is the confident expectation of a desired future condition. Hold out for your promised expectation and don't settle for anything less. You no longer have to walk in fear or lean on the arm of your own understanding of your present circumstances, just hanging by a thread, but you have this hope, the assurance that rests upon the promises of God through Jesus Christ. He is your rope of hope!

For I consider that the sufferings of this present time are not worthy to be compared with the glory which shall be revealed in us. For the earnest expectation of the creation eagerly waits for the revealing of the sons of God. For the creation was subjected to futility not willingly, but because of Him who subjected it in **hope** *. . . Not only that, but we also who have the firstfruits of the Spirit, even we ourselves groan within ourselves, eagerly waiting for the adoption, the redemption of our body. For we were saved in this* **hope***, but* **hope** *that is seen is not* **hope***; for why does one still* **hope** *for what he sees? But if we* **hope** *for what we do not see, we eagerly wait for it with perseverance* [emphasis added].*
— The Apostle Paul (Romans 8:18-20, 23-25)

Bishop Jim Bolin
SENIOR PASTOR, TRINITY CHAPEL

Bishop Jim Bolin is a man after the heart of God.

Along with his wife Robin and their children, Jason and Jessica, Bishop Bolin began Trinity Chapel in 1983 with five other families. Today, the church continues to grow, ministering to over 10,000 people each week.

The principle of "Love, Acceptance, and Forgiveness" is the hallmark of Bishop Bolin's ministry. He has made the mission of Trinity Chapel to extend love, acceptance, and forgiveness to everyone who walks through their doors.

Bishop Bolin has a deep desire to experience a true revival of the power of God manifested through the Holy Spirit in the church today. Trinity Chapel is experiencing a divine visitation of God with salvation, healing, deliverance, and evidence of God's power.

Bishop Bolin attended Lee University in Cleveland, Tennessee as well as Kennesaw State University in Georgia. He serves the Church of God as a member of the Executive Council, World Missions Board, and the Spiritual Renewal Committee. Most recently, Bishop Bolin received his Honorary Doctorate Degree from Jacksonville Theological Seminary.

The people of Trinity Chapel, as well as leaders across the Christian community, have a deep love and respect for Bishop Jim Bolin. He operates powerfully under the anointing of God in the office of Bishop and Teacher. Those that know him will testify of the awesome love and compassion that he demonstrates for people. They will also testify that he is a man that is seeking after God, yielding to the Holy Spirit, open to God's direction in his life, and ready to release the anointing and power of God that has been deposited into his life.